The Bog People

P. V. Glob

THE BOG PEOPLE
Iron-Age Man Preserved

Translated from the Danish by
RUPERT BRUCE-MITFORD
Keeper of British and Medieval Antiquities
in the British Museum

CORNELL UNIVERSITY PRESS
Ithaca, New York

First published in the United States of America, 1969
Cornell University Press

Second printing, 1970
First published, Cornell Paperbacks, 1988

Originally published in Denmark by
Gyldendal as: *Mosefolket: Fernalderens*
Mennesker bevaret i 2000 År

International Standard Book Number
0–8014–9527–X (paper)

Library of Congress Catalog Card Number
69–20391

Printed in Great Britain by
Redwood Burn Limited, Trowbridge, Wiltshire

for

VERONICA	WENDY	PIPPIN
CATHERINE	CATRIONA	SUSIE
ANDREA	JANE	MARY
ELIZABETH	GEORGINA	MIRANDA
PRUDENCE	ILEANA	ELSEBETH

Dog var de skabt af Jord og Ild som vi,
vi er de samme Kraefters Atterkomster,
vi vaagned op af alt, som er forbi.
Paa Dødens Trae vi gror som Nuets Blomster.

Thøger Larsen

Yet they were made of earth and fire as we,
The selfsame forces set us in our mould:
To life we woke from all that makes the past.
We grow on Death's tree as ephemeral flowers.

Contents

Illustrations

MAPS

Acknowledgments are made to the following for the use of photographs:
Harald Andersen; C. H. Vogelius Andersen and A. C. Andersen; Sophus Bengtson; P. V. Glob; Jensen Silkeborg; Carl Krebs and Erling Ratjen; Lennart Larsen; Mainz Zentralmuseum; Carl Neergaard; Per Pejstrup; Albert Sandklef; Georg Sarrauw; Schleswig-Holsteins Landesmuseum; Skabelund, Aarhus; Axel Steensberg; Hans Stiesdal.

An Answer to a Letter

'There is a strange power in bog water which prevents decay. Bodies have been found which must have lain in bogs for more than a thousand years, but which, though admittedly somewhat shrunken and brown, are in other respects unchanged.' So reads a Danish almanack of 1837, alluding to the discovery two years earlier of a woman's body in Haraldskjaer Fen, near the ancient royal seat of Jelling. The finding of this well-preserved woman's body in a bog created a sensation throughout Denmark, more particularly as scholars held that she might be the Norse Queen Gunhild, the widow of King Eric Bloodaxe, who, nine hundred years earlier, had been enticed to Denmark by King Harald with a promise of marriage, but on arrival had been ignominiously drowned in a bog instead.

Nowadays, news of such discoveries in Danish bogs travels round the world—as happened when two Iron Age men were recovered from the bogs at Tollund and Grauballe in Central Jutland some years ago. The scores of letters, telegrams and poems I received from every corner of the world, after the appearance of several articles I had written about them in foreign newspapers and journals, are concrete evidence of this. Nearly all the requests I received—and they were numerous—were for more information about the celebrated bog men, and for more pictures of them. Scholars asked for details. Children wrote thanking me for a thrilling story and saying that they included me in their prayers at night.

Just before I left on an archaeological expedition to the Sheikdoms in the Gulf of Aden in December 1962 I received a letter from a group of English schoolgirls:

> Convent of the Assumption,
> Hengrave Hall,
> Bury St. Edmunds,
> Suffolk,
> England

Dear Doctor Glob,

We were very interested in the Tollund Man. We learned about him in History. We would like to know where he is now because we want to visit him when we are older. We have been told that you are very busy and so we hope you do not mind our bothering you but we would like to know more about him.

As I was just going away my secretary undertook to send over such offprints as I had available in English on the subject. Soon another letter from the young girls arrived:

Thank you very much for the very encouraging pamphlets you sent us. Our set is very interested in History which we like very much. When you sent us the pamphlets it was very encouraging. We think it must be very exciting to look for people in peat bogs. We like hearing about these people because it is amazing how well they have kept.

We are sending with this letter a little book about our school. We hope you will like it. My father has friends in Denmark and I hope he will take us there one day with him. I hope too to have the chance of meeting you and the Tollund man and the Grauballe man. Perhaps you will be coming over here one day?

> Lots of love . . .

AN ANSWER TO A LETTER

Dear young girls,

Home again from the deserts and oases of the Sheikdoms I find your enthusiastic letters on my desk. They have aroused in me the wish to tell you and many others who take an interest in our ancestors about these strange discoveries in Danish bogs. So I have written the 'long letter' in the following pages for you, for my daughter Elsebeth, who is your age, and for all who, like you, wish to know more about antiquity than they can gather from the short accounts and learned treatises that exist on the subject. But I have all too little time, so that it has taken me a long while to finish my letter. However, here it is. You have all grown older and so perhaps are now all the better able to understand what I have written about these bog people of two thousand years ago.

Yours sincerely,
P. V. Glob.
August 13th, 1964

I The Tollund Man

An early spring day—8 May, 1950. Evening was gathering
over Tollund Fen in Bjaeldskov Dal.* Momentarily, the sun
burst in, bright and yet subdued, through a gate in blue
thunder-clouds in the west, bringing everything mysteriously
to life. The evening stillness was only broken, now and again,
by the grating love-call of the snipe. The dead man, too, deep
down in the umber-brown peat, seemed to have come alive.
He lay on his damp bed as though asleep, resting on his side,
the head inclined a little forward, arms and legs bent. His
face wore a gentle expression—the eyes lightly closed, the lips
softly pursed, as if in silent prayer. It was as though the dead
man's soul had for a moment returned from another world,
through the gate in the western sky.

The dead man who lay there was two thousand years old.
A few hours earlier he had been brought out from the shelter-
ing peat by two men who, their spring sowing completed,
had now to think of the cold winter days to come, and were
occupied in cutting peat for the tile stove and kitchen range.

As they worked, they suddenly saw in the peat-layer a face
so fresh that they could only suppose they had stumbled on a
recent murder. They notified the police at Silkeborg, who
came at once to the site. The police, however, also invited
representatives of the local Museum to accompany them, for
well-preserved remains of Iron Age men were not unknown in

* Dale or valley.

1   The Tollund man, who died 2000 years ago

Central Jutland. At the site the true context of the discovery was soon evident. A telephone call was put through straight-away to Aarhus University, where at that moment I was lecturing to a group of students on archaeological problems. Some hours later—that same evening—I stood with my students, bent over the startling discovery, face to face with an Iron Age man who, two millennia before, had been deposited in the bog as a sacrifice to the powers that ruled men's destinies.

The man lay on his right side in a natural attitude of sleep. The head was to the west, with the face turned to the south; the legs were to the east. He lay fifty yards out from firm ground, not far above the clean sand floor of the bog, and had been covered by eight or nine feet of peat, now dug away.

On his head he wore a pointed skin cap fastened securely under the chin by a hide thong. Round his waist there was a smooth hide belt. Otherwise he was naked. His hair was cropped so short as to be almost entirely hidden by his cap. He was clean-shaven, but there was very short stubble on the chin and upper lip.

The air of gentle tranquillity about the man was shattered when a small lump of peat was removed from beside his head. This disclosed a rope, made of two leather thongs twisted together, which encircled the neck in a noose drawn tight into the throat and then coiled like a snake over the shoulder and down across the back. After this discovery the wrinkled fore-head and set mouth seemed to take on a look of affliction.

Proper study of such an interesting find, and the need to preserve it for the future, called for its immediate removal to the National Museum in far away Copenhagen. Preparations were quickly begun. In the gathering dusk a local saw-mill was visited and asked to supply planks for a box to be built in the bog round the dead man and his bed of peat, so that everything could be despatched for investigation intact. As darkness encroached, this task had to be postponed. Next day a strong team from the Silkeborg Museum moved in under the direction of two Museum curators, Peter Nielsen and H.

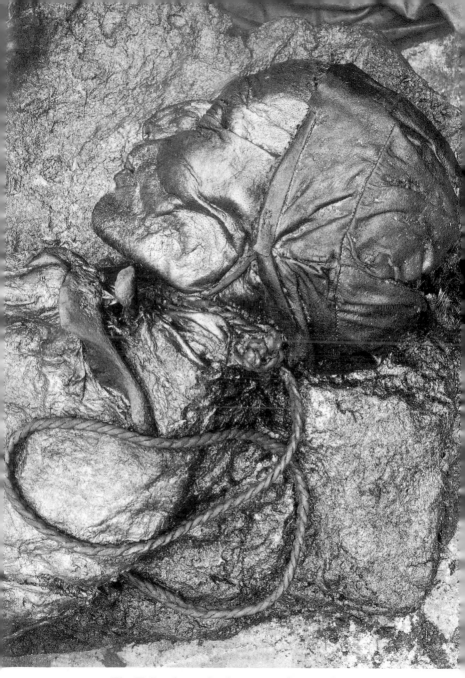

2 The Tollund man in the course of excavation

Hansen, assisted by the police. The dead man and the surrounding peat were first tightly walled in between the sides of the box. Next, boards were pushed in underneath the whole. When the box had been filled right up to the top with peat blocks so that there was no possibility of its contents shifting during the journey, a lid was nailed on.

The heavy plank box weighed almost a ton when filled. It had to be raised nearly ten feet vertically from the bottom of the bog and on to a horse-drawn cart which was to take it to the nearest railway station, in the village of Engesvang. The soft surface of the bog made it impossible to bring a crane up to the spot, and everything had to be done by hand. This was not accomplished without loss. One of the helpers overstrained himself and collapsed with a heart attack. The bog claimed a life for a life; or, as some may prefer to think, the old gods took a modern man in place of the man from the past.

A unique feeling of antiquity still rests over the landscape around Tollund Fen and the Bjaeldskov valley. A ravine with sandy wheel-tracks leads down between high heather-covered slopes to the sacrificial bog, passing through vegetation in which the red trunks and dark caps of fir, and willows—with light golden catkins and slender pointed green leaves in the early spring—predominate. Wild cherry, blackthorn, crab-apple and briar grow on the sloping banks, and with them the ancient Danish forest tree, the aspen, its leaves still shivering from the winter's cold. It is the primeval northern woodland, not very different from the oldest Jutland forests of which we have knowledge.

The valley debouches into the fen, which is still covered with a wild profusion of flora in spite of two thousand years of peat-cutting. The sides of modern peat-cuttings show vertical stripes, the marks made in cutting the good solid peat-mass. In them, however, lighter-coloured areas are to be seen, the smaller-scale peat-workings of earlier ages. It was in one of these that the man had been deposited. A peat-spade made entirely of wood and belonging to the same remote period had

3   The sunken road leading down to the bog where
the Tollund man was found

in fact been found a few days before the discovery of the Iron Age man.

The bog at Tollund opens out into a great tract of fenland, the old Bølling lake, now grown over, and reflecting the blue sky no more. Some of Jutland's earliest hunters once lived on its shores. In the north of the region lies the ancient hunting station of Klosterlund, about ten thousand years old, and to the south, at Hesselhus, a somewhat later habitation-site with thousands of small geometrically-struck flint flakes belonging to a culture with affinities over wide tracts of Central and Eastern Europe. Ancient burial mounds can be seen in rows on the high ground surrounding the fenland. They mark the line of ancient highways. Some three or four hundred of these bowl-shaped memorials of the distant past once existed in the immediate neighbourhood. Only a third of them still survive in the grass and heather, or overgrown with trees. These mounds date from the Stone and Bronze Ages and are therefore between one and two thousand years earlier than the Iron Age man. The oldest are the funeral monuments of the 'battle-axe people', who invaded Eastern and Central Europe about four thousand years ago from the far-off steppes of Central Asia. Some branches of these people penetrated as far north as Jutland and settled there. They were of Indo-European stock, and it was their incursion into the Scandinavian lands so long ago that more than anything else gave the northern peoples the special physical characteristics which persist to this day. The battle-axe people formed a solid foundation in these regions for the development of the culture of the period which followed—the Bronze Age, in which bronze was the most important metal for weapons, tools and ornaments.

The Tollund man represents the population of the succeeding period, the Iron Age, in this area; but he is not the only Iron Age man from these bogs. In June 1938, again during peat-cutting, and only sixty yards further out in the bog to the north-east, a remarkable discovery had been made—a man wrapped in an animal skin. Because of the skin, the peat-cutters at first thought they had come upon a roe-deer and continued digging until they saw woven material. Only then was the assistance of the National Museum called for. By this time the legs and lower part of the body had been almost completely dug away.

This dead man lay about five feet below the surface of the fen, with his head to the south and his legs to the north. It was clear that he lay in an old excavation in the bog, probably an ancient peat-working. The way in which the hair was dressed was interesting. Locks from the forehead and neck were gathered up in a knot on the left side of the back of the head. The animal skin in which the man was wrapped was some kind of sheepskin with pieces of cow hide sewn on to it. A leather strap, about sixteen inches of which were preserved, was threaded through a buckle; and this suggested that the man was either strangled or hanged before being deposited in the bog. The woven material which had led to the suspension of peat-cutting turned out to be a belt twenty-six inches long and about one and a half inches wide.

Yet another body was found in May 1898 in a little bog two and a half to three miles further north. This, however, will be described later.

A rich find of gold of Iron Age date occurred in the same district near the ancient highway, marked by prehistoric burial mounds, along the terminal moraine of central Jutland, where, twenty thousand years ago, the edge of the ice-cap remained stationary for a long period during the last glaciation. The find, at Stenholt, comprised ten gold discs with representations of a dragon-like bird, five pieces of ring-money, eighteen glass beads and a bar of silver. Such a discovery tells us that this highway already existed in the Early Iron Age. It was still in use throughout the Middle Ages, following the same track. The pilgrims' way from distant Iceland to the Holy City of Rome also followed this route, and it has remained in use up to our own day as a drove-way for cattle to the south. The two Romanesque parish churches of Kragelund and Funder have fine granite sculptures: Christ

4 *and* 5   The Tollund man completely uncovered

blessing, animal figures resembling lions and dragons, and runic inscriptions. These inscriptions name the patrons and builders of the churches and, together with some of the animal representations, establish similar links between the use of this highway and the final pagan phase of the Iron Age.

The name Tollund, which appears in the form *Torlund* in a document of 1481, may have ancient origins. It probably indicates a grove sacred to one of the best-known gods of the Viking age, Thor, described in the *Poetic Edda* as the strongest of all gods and men. Thor is the sky god, Asiatic in origin. His symbol is a hammer, the handle of which he grasps with iron gloves. He derives the power he uses in hurling it at his enemies from a special belt which doubles his divine strength when he fastens it round his body. When he moves from place to place, in a waggon drawn by a team of goats, the heavens thunder. He wishes all men well and stands by them in the face of their enemies and against the new God, Christ. 'Tor's Grove', however, was not situated where the bog lies in Bjaeldskov Dal, but probably near Tollund farm, closer to Funder Kirkaby.

The journey of the Tollund man by rail through Denmark took a week. As soon as he reached the National Museum's laboratory in Copenhagen a thorough investigation was begun under Dr Knud Thorvildsen, the head of the laboratory. The long journey had gone well. When the plank box was taken apart the dead man was found lying on his peat bed exactly as when he was first uncovered. Examination of the block of peat which surrounded the body confirmed that he had been deposited in an old peat-cutting at some time in the Early Iron Age, that is, about two thousand years ago. Underneath the whole body was a very thin layer of sphagnum moss, a reddish peat-stratum which was formed in Danish bogs precisely in the Early Iron Age. Danish peat-cutters call it 'dogs' flesh' because of its colour and its relatively poor quality as fuel.

The Iron Age man's head and body were exceptionally well preserved, particularly the side which lay downwards and so was first subjected to the action of the bog water. Bog water,

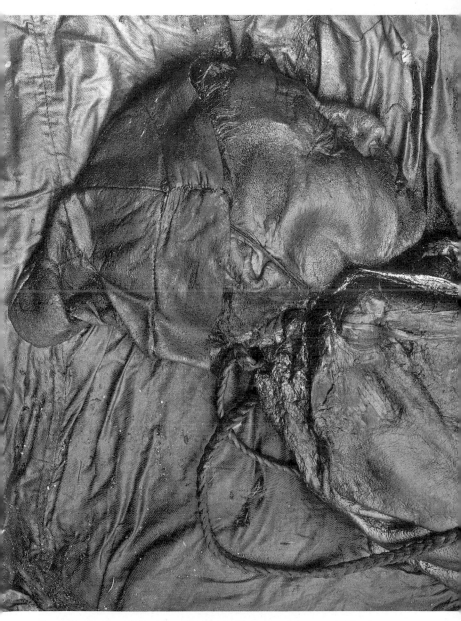

6 'The dead and the sleeping, how they resemble one another'

saturated with soil-acids, is an essential factor in the preservation of this type of ancient find. If the soil-acid is not too strong, the bones are preserved. On the other hand, they may disappear completely in certain circumstances, dissolved in the water by the action of the acid and further decalcified by the roots of bog plants. This point is illustrated by a find made at Damendorf, in Schleswig. Here only the skin survived; but it was so well preserved that it might have been taken from a living man.

The Tollund man's head was especially well preserved, the best-preserved human head, in fact, to have survived from antiquity in any part of the world. Majesty and gentleness still stamp his features as they did when he was alive. His cropped hair, up to two inches long, was not dressed in any way. His eyebrows were partially preserved, and the very short stubble already mentioned covered his upper lip, chin and cheeks. It is the dead man's lightly-closed eyes and half-closed lips, however, that give this unique face its distinctive expression, and call compellingly to mind the words of the world's oldest heroic epic, *Gilgamesh*, 'the dead and the sleeping, how they resemble one another'.

As to the condition of the body, Dr Thorvildsen writes that most of its upper part was still covered with skin. The left part of the chest and the left shoulder, however, were slightly decomposed, the epidermis being absent from considerable areas. A succession of sharp cuts could be seen down the back. These had been caused by peat-cutting. The left hip-bone protruded from the skin and the stomach lay in folds. The sexual organs were in a good state of preservation.

The naked body was clad only in cap and girdle, with a skin rope fastened tightly around the neck. The pointed cap was made of eight pieces of leather sewn together, the hair side inwards, and was fastened to the head by two thin leather laces, fixed at the temples with knots and tied off in a bow, which was tucked in under the cap at the right temple. The belt lay low on the hips, in folds at the back but tight across the stomach. Made of thin hairless skin, it had one end drawn through a slot in the other and wider end and was secured with a slip-knot on the left side.

The plaited skin rope round the dead man's neck was knotted at one end to form an eyelet through which the other end was drawn, forming a noose which could be tightened from the back. It had left clear impressions in the skin under the chin and at the sides of the neck, but no mark at the nape of the neck, where the knot rested. The rope was skilfully plaited from two strips of hide about half an inch wide, and measured five feet from the curve of the eyelet to the opposite extremity. It had, however, been cut at this point and must originally have been longer.

The Tollund man most probably met his death by means of this rope. The vertebrae of the neck did not appear to be damaged, but the doctors and medico-legal experts who took part in the examination judged, nevertheless, from the way the rope was placed that the Tollund man had not been strangled, but hanged. An attempt was made to decide the point by radiography, carried out by a senior medical officer at Bispebjerg Hospital, Dr Baastrup. The result was indeterminate, because of the decalcified state of the vertebrae. A radiograph of the skull was taken at the same time. This showed clearly that the head was undamaged. The wisdom teeth had developed, indicating that the man must have been appreciably over twenty years old. The brain was intact but shrunken. An autopsy showed that the inner organs such as the heart, lungs and liver were very well preserved. So was the alimentary canal, which was removed by the palaeo-botanist, Dr Hans Helbaek, with the object of determining the nature of the dead man's last meal. This was still contained in the stomach and in the larger and smaller intestines which, though somewhat flattened by the weight of the overlying peat, were otherwise intact.

These organs were carefully rinsed externally, to remove contamination from the surrounding peat. Their contents were then washed out and proved to consist of a blend of finely reduced plant remains and particles of seeds. The contents of the stomach and the smaller intestine were inconsiderable, occupying in volume barely 0.5 and 10 cubic centimetres respectively. The contents of the larger intestine, on the other hand, amounted to 260 cubic centimetres. All was of the same character. It was not possible to establish with certainty the proportions of the different ingredients because the plants had varied in their resistance to the digestive juices which had acted on them from the time the meal was eaten and for some while after death.

By the time it has been crushed in a hand-mill and between the teeth a meal of this kind, consisting largely of grains and seeds, is reduced to myriads of small particles. The basis of the investigation was a sample of 50 cubic centimetres taken from the larger intestine.

In collaboration with the anatomists, Drs Bjøvulf Vimtrop and Kay Schaurup, a point of great interest was established. Investigation showed that although the contents of the stomach consisted of vegetable remains of a gruel prepared from barley, linseed, 'gold-of-pleasure' (*camelina sativa*) and knotweed, with many different sorts of weeds that grow on ploughed land, it could not have contained any meat at the time of death, since recognizable traces of bone, sinew or muscular tissue would certainly have remained. It was further established, from the degree of digestion of the remains of the meal in the alimentary canal, that the Tollund man had lived for between twelve and twenty-four hours after eating his last meal.

In addition to the varieties of cultivated grain, it is worth noticing the unusual quantity of knotweed (*pale persicaria*) in the stomach. It must have been gathered deliberately and other plants represented may have been gathered along with it incidentally; for example, blue and green bristle-grass, dock, black bindweed, camomile and gold-of-pleasure. The gruel made from this mixture of cultivated and wild grains was no doubt the normal diet in the early Iron Age, around the time of Christ, when the Tollund man was alive. Fish and meat were also eaten. Rich furnishings of bowls and dishes, with

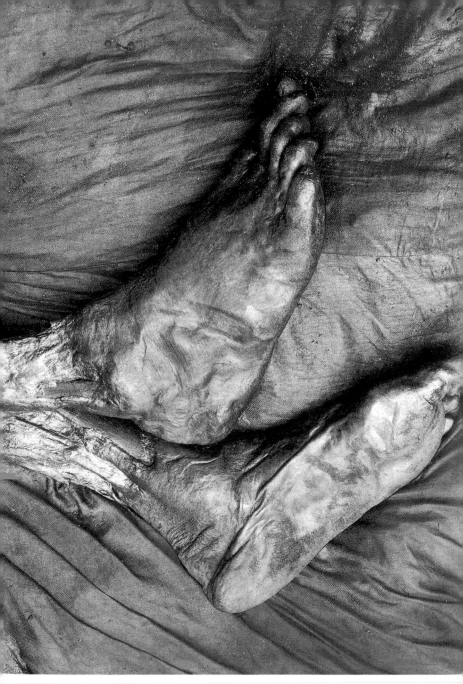

8　The Tollund man's feet

ribs of ox and sheep, and carving knives lying ready, are known in the graves of the time. But meat was certainly not the daily diet as it was in the time of the Stone Age hunters. Milk and cheese, on the other hand, probably were, as the forms of the pottery vessels would seem to indicate.

It is not surprising that this two-thousand-year-old 'recipe' for gruel from the Iron Age (consisting primarily of various cultivated grains together with the seeds of many types of weeds known at that time), should have been tried out in our own day, and in front of a big audience at that. Gruel made to this recipe was served up on an English television programme, in the summer of 1954, to two well-known archaeologists—Sir Mortimer Wheeler and Dr Glyn Daniel. Reports tell us that these gentlemen were not particularly smitten with the taste and had to wash it down with good Danish brandy, drunk from a cow-horn. Sir Mortimer finished up by saying that it would have been punishment enough for the Tollund man to have been compelled to eat this gruel for the rest of his life, however terrible his crime might have been. The Tollund man, though, would not have had brandy to help it down, as the archaeologists did. It was not until about a thousand years later that people learned to distil something stronger from fermented drinks. However, there was an alcoholic drink in the Iron Age, as has been revealed by analysis of sediments in bronze vessels of the period. It was half way between beer and a fruit wine. Barley and the wild plants cranberry and bog myrtle were used in its manufacture. The alcoholic content may have been increased by the addition of honey. This agrees with the account given in the Roman historian Tacitus' *Germania*, a work contemporary with Denmark's Early Iron Age. It says of the Germani that 'they drink a fluid made from wheat or barley, fermented so as to give it some resemblance to wine'.

When the exhaustive study of the Tollund man had been concluded, a decision was taken on preserving him for the future. Unfortunately it was only thought practicable to undertake the conservation of the splendid head. This was first of all placed for six months in a solution of water to which formalin and acetic acid had been added. The solution was then changed for one of 30 per cent alcohol, which was later replaced by one of 99 per cent alcohol to which toluol had been added. Finally, it was put into pure toluol progressively mixed with paraffin, for which wax heated to different temperatures was later substituted. After more than a year's treatment the head was sent to the Silkeborg Museum in Central Jutland, a bare six miles from the spot where it had come to light in Tollund fen. It can be seen there, alongside other discoveries of the Iron Age.

In the process of conservation the proportions of the head and the features of the face were happily completely retained, but the head as a whole had shrunk by about 12 per cent. In spite of this it has emerged as the best preserved head of an early man to have come down to us so far. The majestic head astonishes the beholder and rivets his attention. Standing in front of the glass case in which it is displayed, he finds himself face to face with an Iron Age man. Dark in hue, the head is still full of life and more beautiful than the best portraits by the world's greatest artists, since it is the man himself we see.

II The Grauballe Man

Barely two years had elapsed since the discovery of the Tollund man when I was called out again to another bog find of the same sort. This time it was in Nebelgård Fen, a little over two-thirds of a mile south of the village of Grauballe and some eleven miles east of Tollund. On Saturday, 26 April, 1952, peat-cutters from Grauballe came upon a well-preserved body. Happily this occurred in a locality where everyone knew whom to go to when anything notable was turned up in the soil or found in a bog—the doctor living in Aidt, Ulrich Balslev. Dr Balslev had spent the whole of his working life in this part of Central Jutland, where he was also known as an antiquarian. He at once passed the news of the discovery on to the Museum of Prehistory at Aarhus and from there it was passed on to me. I went out the next day, early on a Sunday morning. The bog lay in the bright, slanting morning light, the dew-drops sparkling like millions of diamonds. A large crowd of the local inhabitants had already gathered. As it was Sunday they had time off from their work on the land. They were tightly grouped in a ring around a dark-coloured human head, with a tuft of short-cropped hair, which stuck up clear of the dark brown peat. Part of the neck and shoulders was also exposed. We were clearly face to face once again with one of the bog people.

The peat-cutters had worked very close to the body both at the head and along its sides. Consequently, it did not take

9   The first picture of the Grauballe man

long to cut away enough of the peat to reveal the bog man's posture and how he lay in relation to the surrounding peat layers, a factor of great importance in determining the period to which he belonged.

It could be seen at once that he lay in an excavation in a very old peat-layer. A soft light-coloured layer of sphagnum moss extended both under and over the body, and showed the line of this excavation, even though its full extent could no longer be established, as its edges had already been dug away on three sides. Well over three feet of the overlying peat had been dug away in that same year. The overlying layer had, however, been much thicker originally. Centuries of peat-cutting, indicated by a sort of honeycombing of the surrounding peat strata, had reduced it, and it had gone to feed the fires of the neighbouring houses and farms.

The Iron Age man lay slightly aslant in the peat, with the head and upper part of the body raised, resting on the bottom of the old excavation. His head lay to the north and his legs to the south. It could be seen already that he lay on his chest, with the left leg extended and the right arm and leg bent. The peat-cutters had completely exposed the head, but in doing so had damaged it to some extent. It had also been affected by the weight of the peat that had pressed down on it for centuries. In spite of all this it serves, like the head of the Tollund man, to give an impression of how this man looked on the threshold of death, many years ago. This time the effect is not one of tranquillity but of pain and terror. The puckered forehead, the eyes, the mouth and the twisted posture all express it. The circumstances that led to his death were probably not the same as in the case of the Tollund man.

When all the necessary observations had been made on the spot a large flat sheet of tin, which had been used for roofing at a nearby farm, was driven into the peat from the side, so that the dead man could be lifted from his damp bed in one piece with the block of peat that still surrounded him. The load was heavy and many of the onlookers had to give a hand before the great block could be lifted on to the floor of a

10 The Grauballe man still embedded in the peat

lorry. It was taken at once to the conservation workshops of the Museum of Prehistory at Aarhus. These workshops were opened some time after the Tollund man had been discovered; otherwise he would have been taken there too. When we had planned the new workshops, however, we had made allowance for future discoveries of this sort, and had had wide emergency doors put in at one end of the building, which might be opened in special circumstances. They were used for the first time that Sunday afternoon when the Grauballe man was taken into the Museum, now his permanent home.

News of the sensational discovery and of the dead man's exceptional state of preservation spread like wildfire. Thousands of people wanted to see the Grauballe man, and after preliminary examination he was placed on exhibition for some days. Long lines of people waited several hours in the queue to see this Iron Age man, almost two thousand years old. Soon, however, his scientific examination had to be resumed.

When the investigation was continued no trace was found of clothing or any object which might have accompanied the naked male body to its resting place in the bog. Garments of skin or of woollen fabric, such as are known from comparable finds, would have been preserved. Linen or other cloth woven from vegetable fibres might have totally disappeared, but, owing to the pressure of the overlying mass of peat, it would probably have left its imprint on the dead man's skin, which was smooth and well preserved almost everywhere. No trace of linen-weave marks was seen. We are forced to the conclusion that this Iron Age man was as naked as the day he was born during the centuries he lay in his bog grave.

There was thus nothing in particular to provide a firm date for the find, only the circumstances of the find itself. These were those of comparable bog finds which could be dated to the earlier Iron Age, the eight centuries between the end of the Bronze Age and the beginning of the late Iron Age—centuries that fall equally to either side of the birth of Christ. It is now possible in archaeology to use a variety of scientific

41

techniques for dating purposes. One technique relies upon the
identification of the flora of the locality at the time when the
man was placed in the bog, so that the climatic phase to which
the discovery belongs may be deduced. Climate changed fre-
quently in past millennia, and the flora changed with it. The
pollen grains of plants and trees present in the different layers
of the bog have to be identified for this method, which is
known as pollen-analysis. A second method, relying on
modern atomic physics, depends on the measurement of radio-
activity, and is known as the carbon-14 method, since it is
concerned with radio-active carbon with the atomic weight
of 14 (C-14).

Pollen grains, though microscopic, are preserved in peat
bogs in a remarkable manner for hundreds and even thousands of years. Since the pollen of every plant has its own
special form, it is possible with the microscope to establish
what plants were growing at different points in time. The
distinct layers in peat-bogs thus become, as it were, the pages
of a great picture-book illustrating the changing flora of the
land through the ages. An exhaustive geological-botanical
study of the Nebelgård Fen was accordingly undertaken by
Dr Svend Jørgensen. We can now visualize the bog and its
surrounding landscape at the moment when the Iron Age man
was deposited in its depths. Dr Jørgensen's investigation included the stratum represented by the block of peat in which
the Grauballe man's body was still encased.

The bog lay then as it does today in a saucer-like depression
in hilly ground. It was covered with a scrub of birch, willow,
mountain ash and alder buckthorn, the vegetation still pre-
dominant when the peat was last cut there. Its surface was
honeycombed with old and new peat cuttings partially overgrown with marsh cinquefoil and cranberry. Bog whortle-
berry flourished on the dry banks around it. The Grauballe
man was deposited in a small peat-cutting which was not
fresh at the time but overgrown. That peat was dug here in
antiquity must have been due to scarcity of fuel. The sur-
roundings had been cleared of woodland, which had only

11 The bog in which the Grauballe man was found

survived in pockets and on precipitous slopes. Oak predominated, while beech, a newcomer in the Iron Age forests, occurred only occasionally, as did lime, ash, elm, fir and alder. Hazel and hawthorn grew at the edges of the forest. Hop was common and the forest floor was carpeted with anemones, dog's mercury, and four-leaved clover. Bracken formed an undergrowth in the glades.

The bog itself was very small and circular with a diameter of some sixty yards, and surrounded by hills that sloped evenly towards its banks. The Grauballe man was found on the south side of the bog about thirty-five yards out from firm ground. Bogs of this type are known as 'cauldron bogs', and it is in just such small cauldron bogs that a long series of the most significant of ancient bog finds have come to light. We will only mention here the *lurs*, those splendid Bronze Age wind instruments, which have been found, in one or more pairs, in such bogs; and, for the early Iron Age, the great silver cauldron from Gunderstrup, with representations of gods and goddesses, religious processions, human sacrifice and contests, which will be discussed later. In both the Bronze and Iron Ages bogs were sacred places at which many religious ceremonies—traces of which we now find in sacrificial deposits—took place.

On the open ground around the bog there were small fields of barley and rye, the same crops as are cultivated there today. Many weeds grew amongst the grain, including knotweed, goosefoot, black nightshade, corn spurrey, field cowwhite and hair-grass. There were large areas of common or heathland which had probably been previously cultivated, but abandoned when the soil had become too impoverished to grow corn, i.e. wheat, barley and rye. A mixed flora of grasses, white and red clover, ribwort, sheep's sorrel, sheep's bit, birdsfoot, trefoil and heather grew on the common. Heather already covered the extensive heathlands of Central Jutland in the Early Iron Age. This flora is that of the centuries that succeeded the birth of Christ, known as the Roman Iron Age because of the strong influences from the great

Roman Empire then apparent in the northern lands. It is in this period, between the year of our Lord's birth and A.D. 400 that the Grauballe man must have been deposited in the bog.

This dating, by means of pollen analysis, agrees exactly with a carbon-14 dating obtained by Henrik Tauber in the carbon-14 laboratory of the National Museum. For purposes of carbon-14 dating, body tissues consisting of the liver and muscle were removed from the Grauballe man before conservation was begun. The radio-activity of these portions of the body was counted in a special type of geiger-counter known as a proportional gas counter, and they were found to contain 81.5 per cent of the carbon-14 content of organisms now living. All living things contain a constant quantity of this radio-active carbon as a result of cosmic radiation from outer space, which produces the radio-active carbon dioxide absorbed by all green plants and by sea-water. From these sources it passes into men and animals, which in consequence become slightly radio-active, a process which only ceases when death occurs. As this carbon content diminishes after death in accordance with very precise rules, it was possible to calculate in the laboratory the time of the Grauballe man's death. Between 1540 and 1740 years had elapsed since he died. This places the date of his death in the final phase of the Roman Iron Age, somewhere between A.D. 210 and 410. A margin of error of plus or minus one hundred years had to be allowed in this calculation on either side of the year A.D. 310. As we shall see, the dating is in full accord with what we can deduce from an analysis of the Grauballe man's last meal, which was still present in his stomach and intestines.

The brief exhibition of the Iron Age man was seen by thousands of people, and resulted in many requests for similar exhibitions in different places. When it was over a series of specialists got down to the investigation proper. A professor of forensic medicine, Professor Willy Munck, carried out the first examination of the Grauballe man as he still lay in the position in which he had been found in the bog. The head, like the rest of the body, was somewhat flattened by the over-

45

12 *and* 13   The Grauballe man after excavation

lying peat, which had pressed on the dead man with its full weight after the water had been pumped out of the bog in preparation for peat-cutting. The skin was a uniform dark brown and as firm as if it had been tanned. This was due to the preservative properties of the bog water, which had from the outset counteracted the various processes of dissolution that set in after death. The hair was found to be preserved on the crown and left side of the head. It was up to about two and a half inches in length and red-brown in colour. However, this was not its original colour, but, like the colour of the skin, was the result of the action of the bog-water. Investigation of the hair seemed to show that it had been dark. Eyebrows were not visible, but there were isolated hairs of the beard on the upper lip and a few more on the chin. They varied in length from one eighth of an inch to almost two fifths of an inch. The eyes, which were slightly screwed up, still contained the eye-balls, and although it was not possible to decide what colour the irises had been, they were most probably fairly dark. Investigation of the bones, which had become soft through decalcification, suggested that they had been intact at the time of death. A fracture of the left femur and tibia, and some damage to the face, must therefore have occurred after death. There could scarcely be any doubt as to the cause of death. A long cut ran round the front of the neck practically from ear to ear, so deep that the gullet was completely severed. The wound was evidently made with several strokes by another person; the direction and appearance of the cuts showed that they could not have been self-inflicted, nor could they have been made after death. As there were no traces on the throat of cord or pressure marks that might have been caused by hanging or strangulation, the cutting of the throat was evidently the cause of death.

Whether the Grauballe man had been knocked unconscious before his throat was cut could not be established. Radiographs taken by Professor Carl Krebs and Dr Erling Ratjen did indeed reveal a fracture of the skull in the region of the upper temple, caused by a blunt instrument, which might suggest a direct blow; but it was no longer possible to determine whether this injury, and also an oblique fracture of the left shin, had been sustained before or after death. However, the radiographic examination showed that incipient rheumatoid arthritis had set in in the spinal column, in the region of the chest. This disease does not usually develop before the thirtieth year, so that an approximate minimum age of thirty is set for the dead man, and this is confirmed by the condition of his teeth. There were no other signs of any illness. Microscopic examination of various tissues, and internal examination in which the lungs and liver were scrutinized, led to no conclusions. In the process of dissection a flat body was revealed in the scrotum—presumably the testicles.

Radiography of the head showed the brain to be remarkably well preserved though a little shrunken. The two halves of the brain can be clearly seen in the radiographs and its convolutions are strongly suggested. The calcium content of the skull had undergone a great change in the bog, but the radiographs still reveal its fine net-like internal structure bounded by the shadow of the surrounding skin.

The study of the Grauballe man's beautifully preserved feet and hands was entrusted to the police laboratory at Aarhus, and carried out by two assistants in the criminology department, C. H. Vogelius Andersen and H. C. Andersen. In their report they describe their astonishment when they looked through magnifying glasses at the Grauballe man's right hand and found that the line-patterns, on part at least of this hand, were clearer than those on their own hands. They confess that their first reaction to the idea that the body was many centuries old was accordingly one of scepticism. Later they realized that they had before them some of the oldest patterns actually preserved in human skin. Like his fingerprints, the lines on the soles of the Grauballe man's feet were as sharp as when they were formed in the embryo, more than one and a half thousand years ago. It was thus possible to take the prints of several of his fingers and of his right foot as well. They would have been quite sufficient to identify him, had he been a modern man and the prints filed in the card index of

14 The Grauballe man's right hand

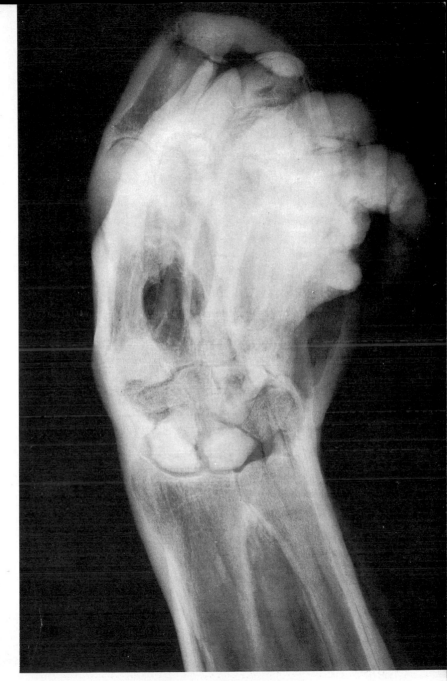

15 A radiograph of the right hand

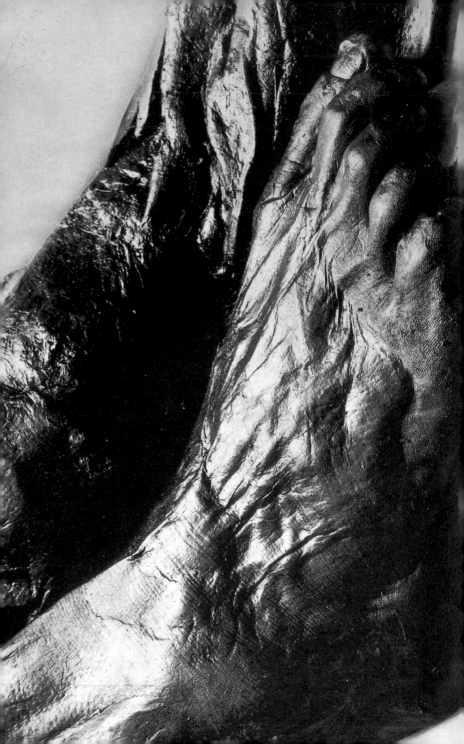

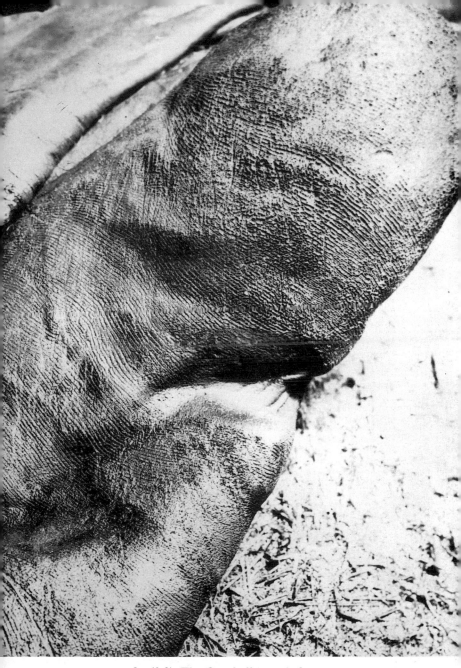

16 (*left*) The Grauballe man's foot

17 (*above*) Its sole

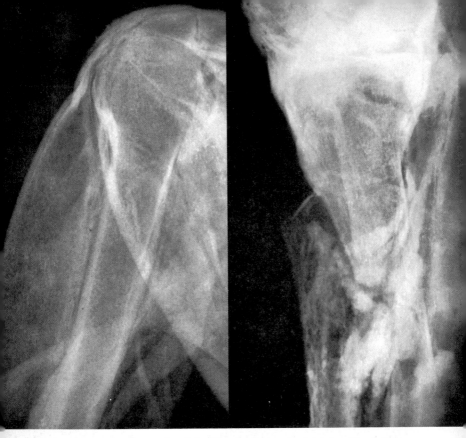

18a, b Radiographs of the Grauballe man's right shoulder-joint, and knee and shin-bone

19 The Grauballe man's finger prints

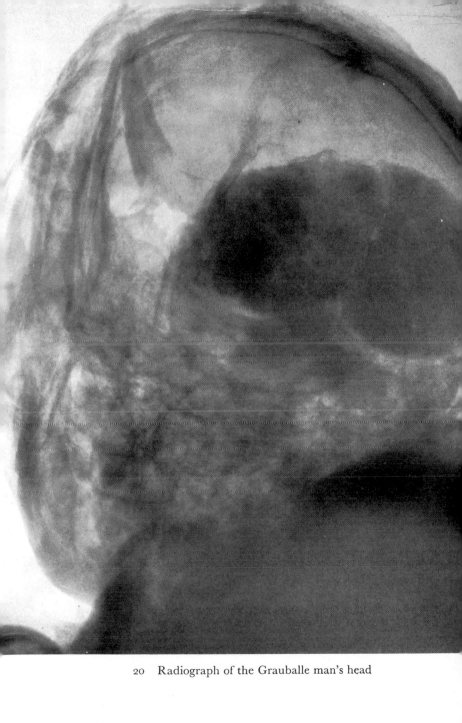

20   Radiograph of the Grauballe man's head

the Criminal Investigation Department. The pattern of the right thumb could be immediately classified as a whorl-pattern, a so-called double-curve pattern, while that of the index finger of the right hand showed an ulnar loop pattern. These two types occur in 11.2 per cent and 68.3 per cent respectively of the present-day Danish male population. The condition of the skin-lines on the hand made it possible to infer that the Grauballe man had never had to do any heavy or rough manual work.

The head had been the first thing to be encountered by the peat cutters and, as already noted, it had sustained some damage. This extended to the teeth, some of which had been driven into the mouth cavity. The teeth were examined by the Director of the Vendsyssel Historical Museum, and by two dental surgeons from Aarhus, Dr Holger Friis and Dr Warrer. Seven teeth were still in position in the upper jaw, and five in the lower, but open sockets for another fourteen teeth were clearly visible, and nine of the teeth were lying loose in various parts of the mouth. The teeth were very small and showed heavy wear and some signs of decay. One tooth had been lost so long before death that its socket had closed up. Several others showed inflammation of the roots, or had holes, which at one time or another must have caused the Grauballe man agonizing toothache. One bad tooth had worked out in such a manner as to interfere with mastication. The wisdom teeth had not come through.

The Grauballe man's last meal was removed from the digestive canal and examined by the palaeobotanist, Dr Hans Helbaek. The bad state of the teeth suggested that the man had not lived exclusively on the type of vegetable diet that this meal represented. The meal had a volume of 610 cubic centimetres, at least double the amount which had remained in the stomach of the Tollund man. It must have been eaten immediately before death. It consisted of a gruel even more mixed in its seed content than the gruel eaten by the Tollund man. No less than sixty-three different varieties of grain were represented in all. Over and above the varieties already named in the case of the Tollund man, remains of the following, amongst others, were found: clover, spelt rye, Yorkshire fog, rye-grass, goosefoot, buttercup, lady's mantle, black night-shade, yarrow, wild camomile, and smooth hawksbeard. Many small bone fragments and some mammalian hairs were also found in the stomach, indicating that the soup or gruel, or whatever it may have been, had also contained meat. The bone fragments, however, could not be identified, nor the animal from which the hairs had come. Quite possibly both had somehow got into the grain supply and so had been included in the meal by chance. We are therefore perhaps justified in saying that the Grauballe man's last meal, like that of the Tollund man, and that of the Iron Age man from Borre Fen, of whom we will be speaking later, was entirely vege-tarian (see pp. 32–3 and 91).

In each of these last meals no trace was found of summer or autumn fruits, such as strawberries, blackberries, raspberries, apples or hips: nor was there any trace of greenstuffs. There are thus grounds for thinking that all three men met their deaths in winter or early spring, before everything had come into leaf. From this we may conjecture that the deaths took place at the time of the mid-winter celebrations whose pur-pose was to hasten the coming of spring. It was on just such occasions that bloody human sacrifices reached a peak in the Iron Age.

All in all, there is less reason for thinking that the Iron Age people were vegetarians than there is for the idea that men chosen for sacrifice were given a special meal, made up of the seeds of wild and cultivated plants, before being consecrated, through death, to the deities who controlled the earth's in-crease (more will be said about these deities later). It is clear, on the one hand, that the 'daily bread' of the Iron Age population must have been blended with a great many seeds from wild plants, but on the other hand, as the investigation of the Grauballe man's teeth suggested, it does seem that their diet was not exclusively vegetarian.

When the investigation of the Grauballe man was concluded the question of preservation arose. This had been discussed at length in the Museum of Prehistory at Aarhus, and it was unanimously agreed that the whole of this Iron Age man should be preserved for posterity, and not merely, as in the case of the Tollund man, his head. The task was given to an officer of the Museum, Mr G. Lange-Kornbak, and carried through by him with great skill. The first problem was to devise some means of ensuring that, at the end of the lengthy process of treatment envisaged, the dead man would still have the same bodily appearance and posture as he had when uncovered in the bog. Accordingly, a plaster cast was taken of the man just as he was found. In this way his authentic appearance was recorded, both with his future exhibition in mind and at the same time to provide a necessary check against possible shrinkage in the course of conservation. The cast was taken from the underside of the body, which was given a coating of glycerin so that the plaster should not stick.

In the post-mortem examination of the Grauballe man a section through his skin showed that it had a light-coloured core but dark inner and outer surfaces, indicating that the process of preservation in the bog had been a tanning process, begun by nature. The solution to the conservation problem would be to complete the process. All the relevant problems in tanning technique were gone into afresh with the best experts in this field. As a result a tanning process, known to the trade as 'pit-tanning' was begun on 1 November 1952. In this process oak bark is used. The tanning which had been in progress in the bog for more than fifteen hundred years was not completed in the laboratory until 1 June 1954, and so the final stage took just over one and a half years. Some 1,825 lbs. of oak bark were used, and the solution had to be renewed three times. The actual tanning took place in an oak trough specially designed for the purpose; the metal fittings which held it together were all on the outside so that the tannic acid would not be contaminated by contact with metal.

When the Grauballe man was taken out after his prolonged

immersion in tannic acid, the bark-slime washed off and the body cleaned, his form and outward colour were exactly the same as they had been at the beginning of the process. A section through the skin, however, showed a uniform brown indicating that the process of tanning was now complete.

The final treatment was a month's bath in 10 per cent Turkish red oil in distilled water followed by drying in air, in the course of which gradual impregnation with glycerin, lanolin and cod liver oil was carried out. Finally, collodion (cellodel) was injected into those parts of the body which had best retained their shape. The thorough-going treatment to which an Iron Age man had been subjected was now stabilized.

Since then the Grauballe man has been exhibited in the Museum of Prehistory at Aarhus, where he lies in exactly the posture in which he was found in the peat-bog. We can say this because the surface on which he rests is the plaster cast taken from his body before conservation began. The cast also showed that hardly any shrinkage had occurred in the long process. We can now see the dead man in a glass case in a special room in the Museum, and encounter one of the Iron Age people almost as he was nearly two thousand years ago, when he was deposited in the bog after ritual sacrifice.

.   *   *   *   *   *

Was it really possible that this man, discovered in the peat-bog at Grauballe, and exhibited in the Museum of Prehistory at Aarhus, was an Iron Age man? Could the scholars possibly be right when they said that the bog had preserved him for two thousand years? These questions occurred to many of the twenty thousand who saw the Grauballe man in the brief week for which he was exhibited before the process of final conservation was begun. All of a sudden scepticism became general and spread throughout the country, encouraged by a big Jutland newspaper and a lot of aping chatter in the rest of the Press.

The alarm was sounded by an old farmer's wife in the

Grauballe district. She reckoned that the dead man was 'Red Christian', a peat cutter who had disappeared from the district without trace in 1887, or the year following. A newspaper announced that the farmer's wife had known Red Christian, had been a playmate of his for many years as a child, and, confronted by the bog man, had exclaimed 'That's him all right!' She recognized his features and traces of the consumption from which he had suffered. Letters to the metropolitan newspapers showed that the Jutland capital was split into two factions, those for the scientists and those against. Readers were told that sensational new evidence had come to hand in the last few days which seemed to establish that the 'prehistoric man' was in fact one and the same person as the drunkard, 'Red Christian', who must have fallen into the bog when half-seas-over, nearly seventy years earlier, and been drowned. The green light was thus given for the discomfiture of Science—represented by the writer—which was attempting to pull the wool over the public's eyes. Any fool could see that a man with hair, finger-nails and stubble on his chin, and as well preserved as this one undoubtedly was, could not possibly be as old as they were trying to make the credulous believe. 'Reliable witnesses' were produced without difficulty. A serious attempt was made to prove Christian's identity with the bog man, and a Jutland newspaper came out with the three-column headline: 'Several recall that Red Christian disappeared at the spot where the Grauballe man was found'. There were pictures of a pretty little white-washed cottage with a thatched roof in which Red Christian had lived.

One of the oldest inhabitants of Grauballe was produced to tell of Red Christian's last visit to the inn at Svostrup, after a poaching expedition. This was an old man of eighty-four, who was credited with being an expert because he was very interested in archaeology and had handed in a number of antiquities to the Silkeborg Museum. It was publicly stated that 'quite obviously, notwithstanding his caution', he was of the same opinion as the farmer's wife who had first recognized Red Christian.

More was to come, however, in the battle against the experts. This time it was an ignorant employee of a Jutland local museum who was made the spear-point of the 'pig's phalanx'* with the headlines: 'Expert queries the age of the Grauballe man', . . . 'leaps to the rescue of the local folk in their mistrust of the Grauballe man's antiquity'. His argument? 'The Grauballe man's pale colour made me sceptical at the time, and I am not convinced even now of the antiquity of this famous find.'

Gossip-writers in daily papers throughout the country joined in the fun with a good deal of witty versification: I will only quote one example:

> *They still remember him well in the parish,*
> *But how famous he's now become!*
> *Yet we have to admit his age has been*
> *Considerably overdone.*
> *Yes, Glob must have made a big mistake*
> *When he made his diagnosis,*
> *And now the folk who know what's what*
> *Want to speak out, and tell what they know.*
> *There's monkey business somewhere†—*
> *Glob must admit it's so.*

While the controversy raged the scholars went calmly on with their investigations. The public were looking in particular to a dating from the Carbon-14 laboratory at the National Museum, but this had to wait for various adjustments, as nuclear explosions in 1956 had raised the general level of radioactivity in the atmosphere all over the world.

* svinefylking (literally a 'gathering of pigs'): wedge-shaped battle-formation in an army.
† 'ugler i mosen', literally 'owls in the bog' (originally 'ulver (wolves) i mosen)—an untranslatable nuance. The expression means 'there's been a snag somewhere'. Containing as it does the word 'mose' (bog) its use is particularly apposite in this context. (Tr)

Eventually the dating was issued and announced by the Press in banner headlines, one of which read:

RED CHRISTIAN KNOCKED OUT BY ATOMS.
RADIO-ACTIVE ISOTOPES PROVE THAT
THE GRAUBALLE MAN IS 1650 YEARS OLD.

The bloodless battle was over. People's natural resistance to the incredible circumstances that a dead human being could be preserved unchanged for centuries, 'by the well-nigh miraculous power of iron-containing bog water', was overcome. A man found in a bog had been accepted as a contemporary Jutlander. But he was Early Iron Age man.

III Bog People in Denmark

Peat has been cut for centuries in Danish bogs as fuel for the hearth, giving protection against the cold of winter and heat to cook food. As long as this has been so, well-preserved dark-brown people have suddenly emerged from the peat, to the surprise, terror and wonderment of the peat-cutters. They believed that it was evil incarnate, the Devil, that they were seeing; or they recalled accounts of sinister, unsolved murders in the district, and men vanished without trace. They could hardly imagine that many centuries separated their lives and that of the dead person in the bog. As a result they nearly always notified the police, or some other local authority, and the body was given a second burial amongst Christians in the nearest churchyard. But in the majority of cases the dead people were prehistoric. Many thousands must have ended their days in bogs, for there are records over the last two hundred years of more than a hundred and fifty such finds, not only men but women and children also. Only in a minority of cases do records survive of the circumstances of the find, of clothing or of sex. Still fewer of the finds themselves have survived. Few though they are, the details of such discoveries are nevertheless often graphic and thrilling. Some will be recounted here.

In a local paper from Odense, dated 18 June 1773, an article by Hans Christian Fogh, the local justice for the district of Ravnholt, and a writer, records a bog-find made

Fig. 1　Map of Denmark showing the sites referred to in the text

64

List of sites shown in Fig. *1*, giving the parish and administrative district

Site	Parish	Hundred
1. TOLLUND	Kragelund	Hids
2. GRAUBALLE	Svenstrup	Hids
3. RAVNHOLT	Herrested	Vinding
4. UNDELEV	Holbøl	Lundtofte
5. RØNBJERG	Rønbjerg	Ginding
6. CORSELITZE	South Alslev	South Falster
7. RØRBÆK	Rørbæk	Gislum
8. HARALDSKJÆR	Skibet	Tørrild
9. HULDREMOSE	Ørum	North Rander
10. FRÆER	Fræer	Helleum
11. BREDMOSE	Storarden	Hindsted
12. ROERSDAM	Nærå	Skam
13. BORREMOSE	Års	Års
14. KARLBYNEDER	Karlby	North Rander
15. SØGÅRD	Daugbjerg	Fjends
16. NEDERFREDERIKSMOSE	Kragelund	His
17. BOELKILDE	Svenstrup	North Als
18. LYKKEGÅRDENS MOSE	Fovsing	Sønderhald
19. HØRBY	Hørby	Hindsted
20. STIDSHOLT	Torslev	Dronninglund
21. ROUM	Roum	Rinds
22. GINDERUP	Heltborg	Refs
23. SMEDERUP	Gosmer	Hads
24. HOBY	Gloslunde	South Låland
25. JUELLINGE	Halsted	North Låland
26. RAPPENDAM	Jørlunde	Lynge-Frederiksborg
27. DEJBJERG	Dejbjerg	Bølling
28. GUNDESTRUP	Års	Års
29. RYNKEBY	Rynkeby	Bjerge
30. FOERLEV NYMØLLE	Skanderup	Hjelmslev
31. REBILD SKOVHUSE	Skørping	Hellum
32. BRODDENBJERG	Asmild	Nørlyng
33. SPANGEHOLM	Ugilt	Vennebjerg
34. HJORTESPRINGKOBBEL	Svenstrup	North Als
35. LISBJERG-GRAVPLADSEN	Lisbjerg	Lisbjerg

The finds are numbered in the order in which they are discussed in the book

some two hundred years ago on the island of Fyn. The purpose of his appeal to the public was 'to obtain, if possible, information about a body found in a peat-bog', although the judge himself was convinced that 'it must have lain there for many years', because of the compact layers of peat that had formed above it.

The find was made on 4 June 1773, when a man with a peat-spade struck off a human foot lying at the depth of 'one and a half ells' (three feet) in the peat.

'As they recognized this as human, four men dug off the peat from above, when a fully preserved male body was found, which was seen by me, the undersigned (Judge Fogh) and two others who observed the following: the body lay stretched on its back with both arms crossed behind the back as if they had been tied together, although there was no trace of bindings. The body was entirely naked except for the head, which was encased in a sheepskin cape, on the removal of which it could be clearly seen that the man had a reddish beard and very short hair, which would have been compatible with the wearing of a wig. The skin was intact over the whole body except under the chin, where one could see right down to the bone, and the front teeth seemed to have been driven into the mouth. The body was otherwise whole and intact, and all the limbs were clearly visible, except for the one foot that had been struck off by the peat-spade.' The account goes on to say that a number of small twigs or branches were laid on top of the body and above these again several small sticks laid crosswise, as though to prevent the corpse from floating or from climbing out of the bog.

This account, written the day the body was found, is valuable for its numerous observations. There can be no doubt that this was an instance of a prehistoric man deliberately deposited in a bog. The head was covered with a skin cape or some similar garment, and such garments are known from a long series of comparable finds of Early Iron Age date. His throat, like the Grauballe man's, had been cut; and the body had been covered with a network of branches. What

66

21a, a The first photograph of a Danish bog man,
Nederfrideriksmose, 1st May, 1892

subsequently happened to this discovery is not known. Nothing of it has survived.

The discovery in 1797 in Undelev Fen (south-west Jutland) of a man of short stature, but strong and broad, is nearly as far back. It was again during peat-cutting and this man too was exceptionally well preserved. He had curly red hair and long fingernails, and was covered with two skin capes—an inner, with hair on the inside, and an outer, with the hair to the outside. On one foot was a cowhide shoe sewn at the back with leather strips, instead of thread, and having holes by means of which it could be strapped to the foot. Alongside the body lay three hazel rods. The find naturally aroused much attention and it was conjectured that the man must be a Tartar, or a Gipsy, or perhaps one of the ancient Cimbri. In the hot summer's day, however, the body began to disintegrate, affected by the sun's rays. Such a peculiar smell arose from it that it had to be covered up again. The local authorities had some planks knocked up into a coffin and the next day the dead man and the three hazel rods were buried in Holbøl churchyard.

As the years passed many bog finds went the same way. When the peat-cutters and local inhabitants had gazed at the dead person and marvelled at the 'well-nigh miraculous power of iron-containing bog water to preserve not only all manner of objects of antiquity but even parts of the human body', so well-known today, the corpse was carted to the nearest churchyard and buried there. Only on one occasion, in 1886 at Rønbjerg, in West Jutland, where three discoveries took place in the course of one year, was it arranged that the objects accompanying the body—the sheath for a knife, a cap and a sheepskin coat—should be sent to the National Museum, before the re-burial was carried out.

On two occasions the dead person was dug up again after re-interment. This happened in the case of a find made at Corselitze, on Falster, in 1843. The find itself is outstanding as the only bog burial to yield ornaments—a bronze pin and seven glass beads, which date it to about A.D. 300. It had already been re-interred in the churchyard when the Crown Prince Frederick came to the spot and personally had it dug up again and sent to the National Museum. Crown Prince Frederick, who became King Frederick VII in 1848, had shown an interest in archaeological discoveries from his earliest youth, and had himself undertaken the excavation of ancient burial-mounds. He, more than anyone else, helped to arouse the wide interest in Danish antiquities which has persisted to this day.

The find was made in a peat-bog on the Corselitze estate in the spring of 1843. Of the corpse only the bones and quantities of long fair hair survived, but to judge from the clothing and ornaments, the dead person must have been a woman. A cloth of sheep's wool, fastened by two bands, was wrapped round her, and the bronze pin and seven beads, now preserved in the National Museum, were at her neck.

It was purely by chance that a bog man came to light for the second time in a fen at Rørbaek, in North Jutland, after being discovered the first time during peat-cutting seventy years earlier. When he was found in 1893 it was the head that came to light first. Subsequently a body was uncovered, which was so well-preserved that people thought it must be that of a pedlar recently robbed and buried in the bog. A local small-holder called Ni-Kristian was suspected of murder. However, the people were afraid of this local gangster (who was later convicted of murder by arson and also suspected of murdering several members of his family), and they did not dare report the discovery to the authorities. The body was put into a box knocked together from planks and buried again in the bog. In 1963 when the cultivation of the bog was undertaken, the mechanical plough suddenly disinterred this box. The story of the old find then came out. However, by this time the body was so decomposed that no further examination was possible. Only a few bones, some hair and part of a leather cap were salvaged.

In the last century the most important discoveries of Iron Age people were of two women from bogs in Jutland. The one which caused the greatest stir was the woman found in Juthe Fen, in central Jutland, on the ancient estate of Haraldskjaer, south of Denmark's oldest royal seat, Jelling, in East Jutland. She was said by a certain Professor and several eminent scholars to be none other than the Norse Queen Gunhild, the cruel consort of King Erik Bloodaxe. Historical sources describe Gunhild as a beauty, refer to her love of pomp, and characterize her as shrewd, witty, clever, merry and eloquent, friendly and open-handed to everyone who would do what she wanted, but cruel, false, malevolent and cunning if anyone crossed her. She seems also to have been dissolute and domineering to a high degree. Of the death of Gunhild the Queen Mother, the sources tell us that she was enticed from Norway to Denmark by King Harald on the understanding that he wanted to marry her; but when she arrived, with a stately retinue, she was met by a party of slaves and house-carls whom he had sent against her. After being grossly maltreated she was drowned and sunk in miserable fashion in a terrifyingly deep bog. This would have been about a thousand years ago. The stories of Queen Gunhild's fate, however, are fantasy rather than historical fact.

The learned gentleman who identified the woman in Juthe Fen as Queen Gunhild had accepted the historical records uncritically. He had also assumed that the happenings described must have taken place at one of the ancient Danish royal seats, either Lejre on Zealand, or Jelling on Jutland. Jelling was preferred because the body had turned up near it, only six miles south of the royal site. In due course it was said that King Harald had been the founder of the Haraldskjaer estate. The woman from Juthe Fen was clad in rich garments, but perhaps the decisive point in favour of the identification was that the bog where the discovery had taken place, or at any rate the area around, had earlier borne the name of 'Gunnelsmose', that is 'Gunhild's bog'.

All these arguments were vigorously contested by a young student, J. J. A. Worsaae, destined to become a very famous scholar and the founder of modern Danish archaeology as a

22   View from Haraldskjaer bog, where 'Queen Gunhild' was found

science. Worsaae maintained that it was not historically established that Queen Gunhild had been murdered by Harald Blue-tooth (King Harald), by being drowned in a bog. He identified the discovery as one of a particular group of Iron Age bog finds. The difference of opinion developed into a major dispute, but Worsaae was on good ground and gained much kudos from his part in the controversy. One of his friends, the author C. Hostrup, used this academic feud in one of his student-comedies, *A Sparrow Among Hawks*, particularly in the original form in which it was performed in the Students Union. When it was edited for performance in the Royal Danish Theatre the personal allusions were cut out.

In the play the journeyman-tailor, Peter Raven, frees Queen Gunhild from the bog by pulling up the stake that is holding her down. Gunhild climbs up out of the hole in the bog:

Gunhild: *O! What a relief!*
The cool night air plays on me
and cools my burning cheeks,
fills my exhausted lungs with fresh life.
Ah, there you are, once again,
you green-crowned woods,
and you, gentle sky!

Raven: *May I take the liberty of asking,*
but did you really come from down there?

Gunhild: *Deep, deep down there I lay, buried alive,*
chained between life and death, in
ignominious torment,
crushed by the weight of earth,
tired of moaning 'air, air'!
and finding no relief
while the years and centuries passed.

Later Gunhild tells why it was that the grim fate of being pegged down in a bog befell her:

They saw me as a troll-wife, come to waste
the land, to injure man and beast
to stir up strife betwixt their kith and kin.
Here was I drowned, and this stick carved with runes
kept me pinned down, for all my Crown,
my magic arts, my anger, in this hole,
where worms in darkness dwell and, through the walls,
the waters of the bog seep in.

The poet Steen Steensen Blicher also made use of this bog find as a theme for his poem *Queen Gunhild* written in 1841. The opening verses run as follows:

Then

Then you were clothed in marten and sable,
decked with precious jewels
gems and pearls in your golden hair
evil thoughts in your mind.

Now

Now you lie naked, shrivelled and foul
With a bald skull for a head
Blacker far than the oaken stake
That wed you to the bog.

Like thousands of others, the poet-priest Blicher had probably seen the supposed Queen Gunhild in the Church of St Nicholas in Vejle, where the body was taken and displayed. Everyone, including those in the highest circles, was thrilled and at the same time smitten with superstitious awe by this find, and King Frederick VI personally presented the oak coffin in which the woman from Haraldskjaer Fen rests to this day in a chapel in the same church. The loose hair, the remains of clothing and the other bits and pieces that belonged to the find were sent to Copenhagen for examination.

This remarkable discovery at Haraldskjaer was not made, as almost every other bog find of this kind has been, on a bright spring day, with plants and trees coming into bud and leaf; nor in the lush green of early summer—but on a dark day in autumn, 20 October, 1835. The discovery was made during ditching. Workmen were digging a boundary ditch across the fen when one of them noticed a human arm and foot appearing at a depth of less than three feet below the ground-surface. No further investigation took place that day, but the next day an unsuccessful attempt was made to get the body out by pulling on the limbs. The reason for the failure was not at first understood, for the body seemed to lie in soft turf. Closer examination, however, revealed that the body was fastened to the underlying peat by wooden crooks, driven down tight over each knee and elbow joint. In addition, strong branches had been fixed like clamps across the chest and lower abdomen, their ends similarly held down by wooden crooks, so that the dead person lay pinned in the bog, the head pointing east and the face towards the setting sun. When the crooks and clamps were removed and the very well preserved if mummified body was lifted, it was at once seen that this was a woman, with long glossy brown hair. The disintegrated garments connected with the body, and the wooden crooks and branches, were collected on the same day, and other items were found in further excavation at the spot on 5 December. The water-level in the bog began to rise, however, and the weather in these darkest months of the year was bad. Further activity was postponed to a more favourable season.

The investigation was not continued until 3 June of the following year. The spot where the dead woman had lain was marked out in an oblong rectangle of at least a hundred and twenty square feet, all the peat in this area being dug out and examined to a depth of nearly ten feet. The bottom of the bog was then traced with a fourteen-foot pole, which sank almost completely before the firm bottom was encountered, showing that the total thickness of the peat-layer at the spot was about twenty-two or twenty-three feet. When the pole was extracted a powerful spring welled up from the depths in a strong jet of water. The only yield from these activities was eight pieces

23 Stakes and branches that pinned 'Queen Gunhild' in the bog

of crooks and branches of the same sort as those which had held the corpse fast in the bog.

The idea behind the fixing of the dead woman in the bog with these wooden crooks and stakes—assuming that she was indeed dead when she was brought there—was explained clearly in an almost contemporary article in the little weekly publication *Light Reading for the Danish Public*. The second issue, dated Friday, 8 March 1839, carried a piece about the discovery under the heading 'The disinterred corpse'. After a description of the find, the article goes on to say: 'Every countryman will immediately recognize in this corpse the body of someone who when living was regarded as a witch and whom it was intended to prevent from walking again after death. Many of us have either ourselves seen, or have heard old people speak of, stakes standing here and there which have been driven in in earlier times, since men first recognized the existence of such restless spirits, by those who, having read of these matters in magical books, thought that by this means they could get the better of the ghosts. Our fore-fathers believed that so long as the stakes stood the ghost remained pinned in the ground. If the stakes were removed, however, trouble would start all over again. The big oak stake is certainly in favour of this explanation. On the other hand the crooks that have survived, and the spot itself, indicate that the dead person met death in a violent manner, perhaps even being buried alive.'

Fear of ghosts has persisted into even more recent times in some parts of the country. There used to be an absolute plague of ghosts at certain times on a hill at Dynved, in the north-west of the island of Als. As luck would have it, about fifty years ago, there lived on the other side of the straits of Als, on the Jutland mainland, a clergyman strong enough to cope with this state of affairs. One day he appeared on the hill with a heavy oak stake and a hammer, walked around for a while on the hillside and finally drove in the stake at a spot where there was nothing in particular to be seen. From then on peace reigned on the hill. Forty years later a museum official, J. Faben, from Sønderborg Castle, undertaking an investigation of the hill for quite different reasons, came upon a thousand-year-old Viking grave. The Viking's breast was still transfixed by the point of the stake which the clergyman had driven in. When the stake was planted it had, of course, been long forgotten that a Viking's grave existed on the hill, yet it was the clamour of this heathen soul which had been disturbing the sleep of the good Christian folk of the neighbourhood down to our own century.

The objects from the Haraldskjaer discovery that were sent to Copenhagen were investigated by the leading experts of the day. The body remained at Vejle and was examined there.

The wooden objects included a heavy stake some twenty inches long, the head of which still bore the hammer marks from when it was driven down into the bog. The crooked sticks were of a very light wood, the kind of willow used in plaiting baskets and wattle fences. The biggest piece was rather over twenty inches long with a crook almost half as long.

The woman from Haraldskjaer Fen, like the other bog bodies, was as dark as brown leather and very well preserved, externally. After drying out she measured five feet two inches in height. Her long hair appeared to have been originally light in colour, perhaps a light brown or golden red, or perhaps grey. Her teeth were all preserved but heavily worn, as is usual with human teeth that have survived from antiquity. This wear is due to the fact that diet consisted mainly of vegetable foods ground on stone querns, and particles of stone became mixed with the food. The woman's skin was much wrinkled, which indicated that she had been rather plump, as did her well-preserved breasts with very large nipples. She must have been about fifty years old.

It was deduced that the woman had met a violent death, and had been pinned down into the bog alive. Her left knee showed a big swelling at the point where it had been fixed down by the long crook, and the expression on her face was 'clearly recognized as soon as she was taken out from the peat as one

24 The Huldre bog, at Ramten

of despair'. Her small hands and feet indicated that she was a person of distinction who had not had to do hard work.

The fragments of cloth found with the body had been woven from sheep's wool. One piece had a fringe along one edge and a lozenge pattern was woven-in in dark thread. A skin cape of reddish-brown leather, probably sheep or cow-skin, was made up of many small pieces neatly and regularly stitched together. There was a cap or head-gear in the form of a fine net in bonnet-style. Unfortunately no information exists as to the original arrangement of these remains of clothing in relation to the body.

The most complete woman's costume of Iron Age date that we have comes from Huldre Fen, at Ramten in Djursland, the broad peninsula which projects east from the mainland of Jutland. The bog itself is a little elongated cauldron-bog lying between hills crowned by ancient tumuli. Although almost wholly exploited by peat-cutting it still retains something of the atmosphere of a sacrificial bog. Reeds and rushes cover its banks and islets; slender birches, alder and willow frame its waters, and endow it with a sense of mystery which the name, Huldremose, increases. For a *huldre* is a kind of fairy, ravish-ingly beautiful to outward appearances but in reality hollow, who entices hunters and lone wanderers with the illusion of love and happiness. But she is a troll and so always dangerous. Any man who is bewitched by the *huldre* becomes spell-bound, yearns for her night and day and finally loses his senses and his life, unless he is set free by some 'wise man'. The road from the village of Stenvad to Ramten passes close by this bog. We may be sure that many a young man in bygone days saw the fairy's mocking dance and heard her entrancing song, even if the actual name of the bog, Huldre Fen, is probably new, the product of the imagination of the local people, stimulated by the recovery of the *huldre* or fairy's body from the bog a little less than a century ago.

For here it was, in 1879, during peat-cutting, that a woman's body was found, surrounded by a considerable quantity of clothing. She lay on her back with her head to the west and her feet to the east. Her legs were drawn up towards the lower part of her body. The right arm was broken off, the left bent across the chest and held tightly to the body by a strong leather strap. Next to the skin she wore a lamb-skin cape, and she wore another over the upper part of her body as an outer garment. A check skirt was fastened to the body with a leather strap and a head-scarf or kerchief of the same material, fastened by a bird-bone pin, covered her head and neck. A leather strap, four feet ten inches in length, and a woollen hair-band were packed inside a bladder. In a pocket was a horn comb of an unusual shape probably of the beginning of the early Iron Age, and so dating the discovery as a whole. Also found were woollen strings, one plaited from two threads twisted together, the other drawn through two amber beads; and 'a fence-post of willow-wood'—a willow stake about three feet six inches in length and some one and a half to two and a half inches thick—lay obliquely across the dead woman's breast.

The woman and the clothing were sent to the National Museum for study. The surviving items of dress are exhibited there now. On a later occasion a further garment was recovered from the bog close to the spot where the woman had been found.

A number of discoveries of women's bodies from bogs in north Jutland remain to be described. One such body, in Auning Fen, had a skin cape and woollen skirt, and was accompanied by various sticks and wooden crooks, which suggest that she had been pegged down like the woman in Haraldskjaer fen.

One July day in 1842 a peat-worker in Fraeer Fen struck the foot of an adult female body lying 'at a depth of two ells' (four feet). It was later extracted from the fen under the supervision of a priest. The woman lay face downwards. With her was a woven woollen garment, and this, together with a shoe with the foot still inside it, was sent in to the National Museum. The shoe was made of two thicknesses of leather, a thinner layer with the hair to the inside, and a thicker with the hair

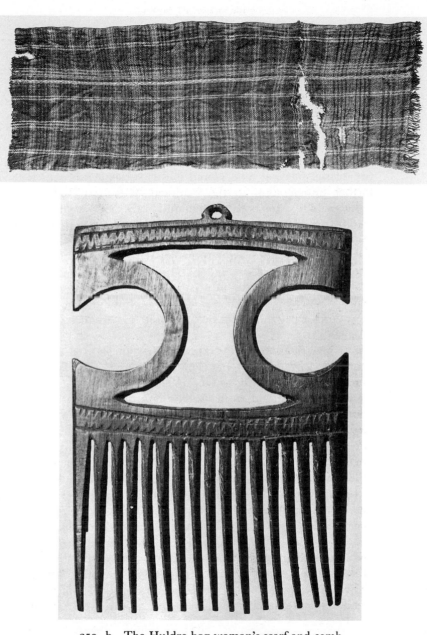

25a, b The Huldre bog woman's scarf and comb

to the outside, stitched together with hide thongs. It was held over the foot by a leather strap and to the ankle by a hide lace.

A discovery made in June 1942 in peat-cutting at Bred Fen, Storarden (Arden forest), is from the same district. As often happens in such cases the local police were first called in, and the body was dug up and laid out in the nearest barn. It was only later that the local archaeologist, the curator of the Museum in Aalborg, Peter Riismøller, was told. He vetted the find at the spot at a meeting with the chief of police and the district medical officer, and it was subsequently sent for further investigation to the National Museum. The peat-cutters said that the body when found in the bog was 'doubled up like a question-mark', and wrapped in cloth so that only the head showed. It had lain in the soft red peat-layer known as 'dog's flesh'. Subsequent geological study of the bog showed that the corpse could not be earlier than the beginning of the Early Iron Age, and was probably somewhat later. It seems, then, that this body, like the Grauballe man and several other bog men, had been deposited in an ancient peat-excavation.

The investigation at the National Museum showed that the dead woman had lain on her right side on part of the clothing. Her legs were so tightly drawn up that the thigh bones were parallel with the body and the feet on a level with the hips. The hands were touching the shoulders. The hair was of a darkish blonde colour and of luxuriant growth and plaited into two pig-tails which were coiled up into a crown on top of the head and bound with woollen yarn. Over the hair was a skil-fully-made little bonnet or cap of wool yarn, held by two fastening-strings. This is made by means of a special technique known as 'sprung' (*sprang*) and is a charming net-like head-covering. Remains of cloth lay around the dead woman but we cannot now say with certainty how this was arranged. Under-neath her at her left side lay a coarse woollen cloth consisting of two pieces sewn together; a long piece of cloth of a finer weave, and, at the head, a decomposed scarf or kerchief.

Anatomical examination showed that this was a young

woman, twenty to twenty-five years of age, and five feet five and a half inches tall. There was no external sign of violence. To judge by the peat-cutters' account she had been brought to the bog, naked and trussed, lying on the thicker cloth and covered by the thinner cloth: the body thus gave the impression of being wrapped in two layers of cloth.

An account of 1836 records a bog find on the island of Fyn: 'In the course of peat-cutting at Roersdam, in Hede, New Odense, some twenty years ago, the well-preserved body of a young woman was found. The garments it wore consisted of deer-skin, very roughly-prepared and not sewn up with thread, but only partially held together with skin laces, like similar garments amongst raw, uncivilized peoples. This body, and the clothing found with it, is preserved in St. Knut's Church in Odense.'

The cutting of peat for fuel has gone on in Danish bogs for over two thousand years. This exploitation of the local fuel reserves, however, was enormously intensified in the years during and following the last world war. Many significant discoveries of antiquities resulted. The finding of the Tollund and Grauballe men have already been described in detail. In the fen of Borre, in Himmerland, a bog body was found in each of the three successive years 1946 8. As all of them were sent for more detailed study to the National Museum good records are available. It is especially interesting that as many as three Iron Age men should crop up in this particular fen, for other finds of unique character and of the same date have come from it. The fen itself is a large one, and the three bodies were separated from one another by distances of some five hundred and a thousand yards. A single sacrificial site or place of burial is thus not in question. A low threshold at the northern end of Borre Fen separates it from the little bog, the Raeve Bog, where the matchless silver vessel known as the Gundestrup cauldron was found in 1891. Its depictions of gods and goddesses, religious processions, animal combats and human sacrifice have already been briefly alluded to. At the southern end the Borre Fen contracts and then opens out

26 The Arden girl's coiled hair

27   Her open-work bonnet

again into a smaller fen where an Early Iron Age refuge-fort, with rampart and ditch, has been excavated. This fort later sheltered the buildings of a village also of the Early Iron Age. It is not unlikely that the three bog men spent part of their lives in this village, or took shelter in the fort when danger threatened. They may even have been present when the great silver cauldron was deposited in the Raeve bog as an offering to the gods. But we will go into all this later on.

In 1946 a well-preserved body (the first of the three) was found during peat-cutting in the southernmost part of Borre Fen, in the parish of Aars, about two hundred yards out from the western edge of the bog and six feet deep. A local report reads: 'On Sunday afternoon wild rumours were circulating in Aars that a body had been found in Borre Fen. It was thought to be a case of murder, and the fact that the official machinery of police superintendent and district medical officer had been set in motion no doubt encouraged people to suspect the worst. When the facts came out, however, they proved to be something of an anticlimax, although the discovery is, of course, of great historical and archaeological interest.' The facts were that this was not a common murder of our own day, as the good journalist had hoped, but one of those men of two thousand years ago whose habitation-sites and burial-mounds are so plentiful and familiar in this very district—a far greater sensation, indeed a matter of world interest, one might suppose. It was, inevitably, the highly competent Curator of the West Himmerland Museum in Aars, S. Vestergaard Nielsen, a graduate in theology, who excavated the body. He turned up, most fortunately, at the bog at just the right moment, as he always did when anything unusual emerged from the earth's safe-keeping in any part of beautiful Himmerland. He organized things immediately so that the body was dug out undisturbed in a block of peat, boxed up with planks and sent to the National Museum for examination. It arrived there on 30 May. Its departure from the local railway station was not without its comic moment; the station master would only agree to consigning the crate as a 'corpse', even though it was explained to him that it was two thousand years old. This method of despatch greatly increased the freight charges and attracted incidental expenses including the disinfecting of the carriage used to transport it. We may take the stationmaster's stand as a compliment to the indestructability of this Iron Age man who had died so long before. This was not the first time in the history of the National Museum that such an episode had occurred nor, fortunately, or unfortunately, whichever way one looks at it, will it be the last.

However, we also have an example of the appreciation of a similar discovery in a letter from the United Steamship Company dated 31 May 1879, and addressed to The Museum of Northern Antiquities. It refers to the woman from Huldre Fen, and reads: ' In consideration of the fact that the body which has arrived on board the *Thy* from Grenaa is despatched for scientific purposes the company waives all freight charges on the same, as we have much pleasure in informing you herewith.'

Vestergaard Nielsen supplies important information about the circumstances of the discovery, obtained by him from the peat-cutters. They stated that beneath a solid layer of peat some twenty inches thick they encountered a limited area where the peat mass, right down to where the body lay, was softer than the surrounding peat. The body lay on solid peat liberally strewn with birch branches of varying thickness. The workmen had encountered similar 'holes', the last one not far from the dead man. This shows that here again use had been made of an ancient peat-working in a bog that had become overgrown with birch. Investigation of the peat-layer established that the man was probably put into the bog at the time when the village in the Borre Fen fort was inhabited; that is to say, in the first century B.C.

Closer examination showed that the dead man had been deposited in the peat-working in a sitting position with his legs bent up and crossed. The upper part of the body, twisted to the left, lay tight against the left thigh, the right shoulder

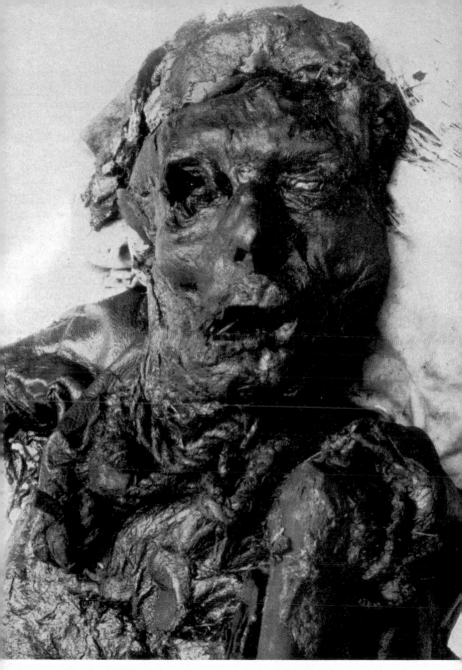

28 *and* 29 The Borre Fen man as he was found, with the halter still round his neck

almost touching the left knee. The head was twisted to the left in such a fashion that the left shoulder had slightly dis-lodged the lower jaw. The arms hung down, the left bent at the elbow, the right lying across the right hip. The body was therefore tightly folded together, perhaps as a result of being buried in a sitting position and then becoming compressed by the weight of the overlying peat.

The dead Iron Age man was exceptionally well preserved. The skin, however, though the pores were all visible, was black and leathery. He was fully-grown, but small in stature, only about five feet two inches in height. The face was some-what damaged, but the nose was particularly well preserved, as was also the left eye which initially was shut but later opened slightly, so that the eye-ball appeared, yellowish-white in colour with a black iris. Only a few head hairs remained. A reddish stubble, about a quarter of an inch long, was spread over the upper lip, chin and neck, indicating that the man had not been shaved on his last day alive. The hands were finely formed, and to judge from the well-preserved left hand in particular he had probably not used them for hard work. The feet were also well formed, with high instep and neatly rounded shape. The back of the head was crushed in, and the paper-thin membrane and the brain mass were visible through a gaping hole in the skull. The right thigh-bone was broken a little above the knee. Investigation showed that these severe injuries were inflicted in antiquity, but they were probably not the cause of death, for round the man's throat was a hemp rope of three twisted strands. It was thirty-eight inches long and about two-fifths of an inch thick, fastened with a slip-knot so that it could be tightened by pulling one end. Both ends were skilfully bound and stitched with hide thongs to stop them from unravelling; they had been longer but had been cut off at the knots. This rope could have been used to hang or strangle the man.

The dead man had been brought to the bog naked except for the rope around the neck. Rolled up at his feet, however, were two capes, sewn together from pieces of light and dark sheepskin. A scrap of woven cloth lay under his head. One of the capes, unusually, had a collar that did up at the neck.

In a post-mortem examination the abdomen was opened and the stomach and intestines were found to be well enough preserved for microscopic analysis, which was undertaken by the botanist, Inger Brandt. The contents proved to be the remains of an exclusively vegetarian meal, the chief elements being corn spurrey and knotweed, both of which were cultivated in the Early Iron Age, and a long series of seeds of weeds, those already familiar to us from the last meals of the Tollund and Grauballe men. The whole was probably eaten in the form of a thick vegetable gruel. Although no other foodstuffs were recognized, their presence cannot, however, be excluded.

Finally, the special character of the discovery was emphasized by the presence of a birch branch three feet four inches long and one and three-quarter inches thick, lying across the dead man.

Scarcely a year had passed before another of the bog people was brought to light in peat-cutting in Borre Fen, this time further to the north-east, and two-thirds of a mile from the previous year's find. The date was 27 June 1947. Fortunately, one of the staff of the National Museum, Elise Thorvildsen, was in the district and she was able to see the find the same afternoon. The dead person lay at a depth of about six and a half feet below the surface of the bog. After preliminary examination the body was removed and sent to the National Museum.

The dead person, probably a woman, lay on her stomach face downwards in an ancient peat-working, her head to the north and her feet to the south. Crucial parts of the body had completely disappeared. The skull was crushed into pieces and the brain-mass visible. The hair was up to an inch or more long and red-brown. Fastened with a granny knot round the neck was a leather strap, on which had been fixed an amber bead and a bronze disc. The body lay naked on a sheet of birch bark. Its upper part was uncovered; the rest was

30 The Iron Age woman from the Borre Fen, in process of being excavated

covered by a sort of blanket, a shawl and various pieces of brown woollen cloth.

The woman may have suffered maltreatment before she ended her life in the bog, for the right leg was fractured four inches below the knee. Directly above the middle of the body lay three sticks, about four inches long, and alongside the upper part of the body some small bones, which could be identified as those of an infant. An unusual and important find was the half of a clay pot, lying on the upper part of the right arm. This, together with geological study of the bog, showed that the woman was contemporaneous with the village in the Borre Fen fort; that is to say, two thousand years old.

The following year yet another discovery was made in the Borre Fen, the body of a plump woman with medium-length hair. Writing to the National Museum on 23 July 1948, Vestergaard Nielsen said of it, 'I have great pleasure in sending you the customary annual bog body from Borre Fen'. This the worthy Curator of the West Himmerland Museum ought not to have said, for no body has been found in the district since. They are now turning up in Central Jutland.

This last discovery was made a quarter of a mile south of the 1947 Borre Fen man, and in the same circumstances. It, too, dates from the time when people lived in the Borre Fen village. The dead woman lay face downwards covered by a large woollen blanket, which was adapted with a leather strap for use as a skirt. The head lay to the east, with the right arm bent up against the face, the left arm was under the left leg which was bent right up underneath her. Like the Borre man and other bog men the woman had been roughly handled before she ended up in the bog. The back of the head was scalped and her face was crushed.

Taking all the finds so far discussed we can see that there are many recurrent features which, in spite of differences in individual cases, link them as a distinctive group of discoveries of the Early Iron Age, the four centuries on either side of the birth of Christ. It would involve a good deal of repetition to

93

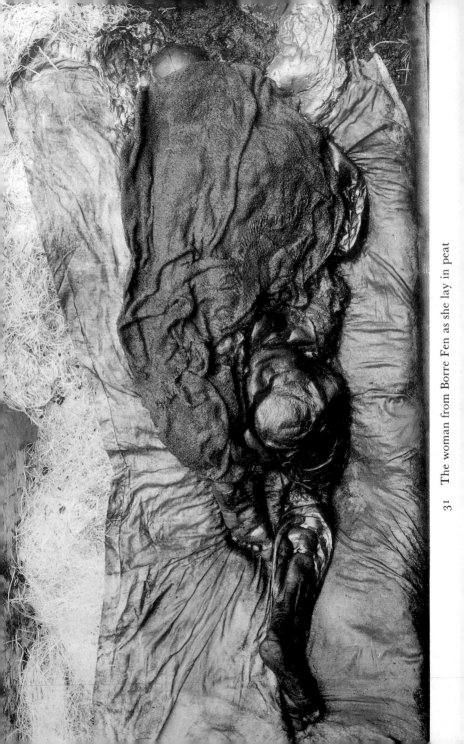

31   The woman from Borre Fen as she lay in peat

32   The woman turned over on her back

set down here what is known of other similar finds, but the peculiarities of some of them may be mentioned.

A man thirty to thirty-five years of age and five feet eight inches tall was found in Søgaard Fen in Central Jutland in 1942. He lay face downwards on an inch-thick bed of bog cotton—the flower with white downy tufts which covers the flat surface of the bog with small shining spheres from mid-summer to autumn. This is the flower which in fairy tales is used to make clothes for kings' sons who have been turned by sorcery into wild swans. With the dead man were a cap, leather sandals and three skin capes. The body was, however, only wrapped in the capes, as had been the case with the man from Kragelund Fen, near Tollund, already mentioned,* not dressed in them. The Kragelund man also wore leather boots fastened across the instep by leather straps.

The item of dress that most often recurs both with men and with women in the bog finds is a short skin cape which covers only the shoulders and upper part of the body. Sometimes more than one cape is found with the same individual, as we have seen. Four capes with one individual, however, which occurred in a bog find of 1900 at Karlbyneder, in Djursland, is unique. Two of these were of sheepskin, one was of lamb-skin, while the fourth was a very elaborate affair. It had a beaverskin collar attached to dog-skin or wolf-skin, while the bottom of the cape was of cow-hide.

Only one Danish find, at Bolkide on the island of Als, yielded two bodies side by side. Remains of rope found with them suggested that they had died by strangulation or hanging.

The most uncanny of the bog-finds are those that consist of a head or just one part of the body, perhaps a hand or a foot. In such instances it would be natural to think that we are dealing with parts of a complete body, the rest of which had been dug up earlier, perhaps centuries earlier, in the peat-cutting which went on all the time. This may also be so in those cases where part of the body is missing. In Lykkegård fen, East Jutland, for instance, a male body with a rope round its neck lacked

* See p. 25.

33 An Iron Age man with a pig-tail, from the same bog as the Tollund man

the left fore-arm. But one cannot be sure that the above explanation applies. A discovery made in Søgard Fen in Central Jutland in 1944 probably represents the remains of an individual originally deposited complete. It consisted of two hands and the lower legs, one with a foot attached, and remains of a skin cape, a short skin coat, and pieces of cloth adhering to the lower legs. In this connection one thinks of one of the women's bodies found in the Borre Fen. It was undoubtedly complete when deposited, but in the years that followed significant parts disappeared. Remains of a skin coat were found with a human foot and lower leg in 1942 in the Tved bog. A human hand, and remains of skin, probably all that was left of a coat, were found in 1945 in Hørby Fen. Both sites are in Himmerland, and as far as we can judge, both finds are the remnants of bodies destroyed earlier during peat-cutting.

It is a different matter with two severed women's heads. One found in 1859 in Stidsholt Fen, in Vendsyssel, is described as the 'somewhat damaged severed head of a (?) young woman of small stature'. The hair was twenty inches long and tied in a knot to which a woven band two and a quarter inches wide and thirty inches long was fastened. It was clear that the head had been struck from the neck with a powerful blow, which had passed between the third and fourth vertebrae and had torn with it a piece of the skin from under the chin. Here we can speak of a genuine case of decapitation, but the date cannot be established, as the woven band no longer exists. We cannot be sure that this is not a head of much more recent date than the Iron Age. It might be that of a young woman guilty of infanticide, the penalty for which was death. In such a case the body might possibly have been buried at the place of judgement itself, while the head ended up in the bog, here exactly on the boundary between two estates, Dronninglund and Horns, in a 'no-man's-land', as we know the practice to have been in later times, when dealing with a person who it was feared may 'walk again'.

On the other hand, the head of a young woman of about

34 The decapitated girl from Roum

twenty, found in June 1942, during peat-cutting in Roum Fen
in Himmerland, dates back to the time of the bog people—the
sheepskin in which it was wrapped was of a kind that is
characteristic of the Early Iron Age. As in so many previous
instances the nearest policeman was called when the discovery
was made. He immediately went to the bog accompanied by a
doctor and a museum official, who made sure by further
excavation that there were no remains nearby of a body to
which the head had belonged. The identification of this head
as a woman's rests partly on the absence of beard stubble and
partly on the wavy reddish-coloured hair, four to five inches
long. The face is very delicately formed, and oval. The teeth
are well preserved, but heavily worn. The head was severed
from the body at the level of the second and third cervical
vertebrae. This severed woman's head was probably a
sacrificial offering. It was found in a little cauldron-bog from
which ancient clothing and artefacts, deposited as sacrificial
offerings to the divine powers, had been recovered earlier.

IV Bog People in Other Countries

It is not only in Denmark, and in North Jutland especially, that people from antiquity have come to light, well preserved after centuries in the peat. They have been found in many other countries too. Dr Alfred Dieck, of Hanover, has listed finds of this kind for the whole of Europe. His list reveals an interesting distribution.

When all old records are taken into account, Denmark will be shown to have produced 166 bog people, and Schleswig-Holstein 69. The figures for the neighbouring areas of North-West Europe are 5 for Hamburg, 141 for Lower Saxony and Bremen, and 48 for Holland. Then come England and Wales with 41, Scotland with 15, and Ireland with 19 finds. Norway and Sweden have produced 9 and 16 bog bodies respectively. As Dr Dieck has recorded 690 bog bodies in all, out of which the foregoing account for 529, only 161 remain for the whole of the rest of Europe. More than half of these come from Central and West Germany. It is thus apparent that these remarkable discoveries have been principally made in North-West Europe. By far the greater part of the ones that can be dated are from the period between 100 B.C. and A.D. 500. Isolated finds, however, go right back to the Mesolithic period, and so are more than 5,000 years old; whilst the most recent are of our own times—for example, Russian and German soldiers killed in the Masurian lakes region in the first world war, and airmen brought down during the last war.

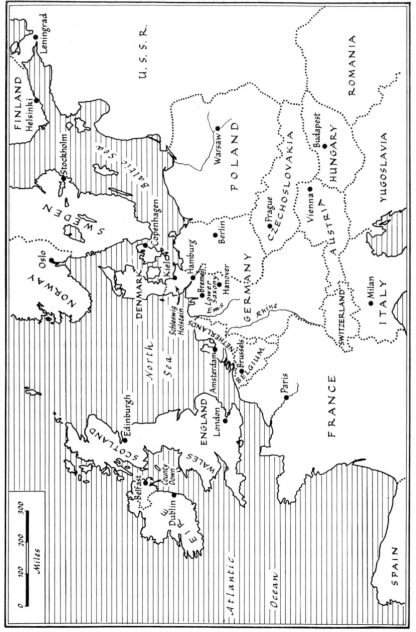

Fig. 2. Map of Northern Europe, to be used in conjunction with Chapter IV

The state of preservation of the discoveries admittedly varies greatly; but in all cases it is the acid in the water, combined with the total exclusion of air, which has tanned the skin and hair of the bodies and so preserved them for centuries. Broadly speaking, the state of preservation ranges, as it does in the Danish finds already described, from outstandingly good to very bad.

The first recorded discovery of a bog body was in 1640, in Shalkholz Fen in Holstein. Since then they have turned up, from time to time, in various places all over North-West Europe, to the surprise and puzzlement alike of their discoverers and of the spectators who always quickly gathered. Out of so many examples we can only discuss those which enlarge our knowledge of this group of finds in some interesting way, or are especially notable.

The first properly documented account of a bog body comes from County Down in Ireland. It is written by Lady Moira and tells us that in the spring of 1781 Lord Moira sanctioned an investigation on one of the farms on his estate from which his factor had brought in a plait of hair found the previous autumn on a human skull. The place of discovery was a small peat bog on Drumkeragh Mountain. Right at the bottom of this bog, on a gravel layer and under a thick bed of peat, lay a skeleton with its head to the east and feet to the west. At each end of the skeleton a rough unhewn stone had been placed. The skeleton was that of a 'very small woman', and on and around it were numerous garments. The peat-cutter who made the find said that he had immediately re-buried the skeleton, but that visitors had taken the best of the garments, and he had only been able to keep the coarsest cloth. Lady Moira writes that she first secured the coarse cloth, but later, having paid well, she obtained another lock of hair and some cloth of finer quality, including a fine piece of a green colour and some of red. The individual garments were said to consist of one known in France as *l'aumusse*—a skirt, made of a skin which could not be identified, since it was in a very bad state of preservation; and an outer garment, a sort of cape worn on one shoulder and passing under the opposite arm. This cape was worked in different materials and colours and had a border into which motifs were woven in a fine technique. It was supposed to have come from the East, and to have been brought in by the Phoenicians. In addition to these items of clothing the account mentions three woollen rugs, one of which lay over the dead woman; ornaments found on the skull, and belonging to a diadem or something similar; a veil of light fabric which lay over the face and, finally, a larger garment on which the body had lain.

Who this lady of high rank was can, of course, be only a matter of guesswork, for the find no doubt dated from the remote past. It is hardly surprising that she has generally been supposed to be a Danish Viking.

In the great fen region to the west of the River Ems eight bog men have been found, at one time or another, on German and Dutch soil. One of these came to light west of the village of Landegge, where an entire family—man and wife, son and grandfather—were peat-cutting on 8 June 1861, laying in the winter's supply of fuel as the family had been doing in this part of the fen for twenty-four years without anything unusual occurring. They were working at a depth of five feet when the grandfather cut in two a worked stick with an incision in one end. When the rest of the stick was pulled out, he said: 'There's a sheep under it.' Closer examination showed that it was a human being, a naked man lying face downwards in the peat, his right hand beneath his shoulder and the left hand down by his side. The legs were bent, so that the lower legs were tilted upwards, but the sole of the right foot only was visible, for the left foot had been struck off. This must have happened at some earlier period since a search failed to reveal it.

The face was astonishingly well preserved—so well, the finder said, that if he had known the man in life he would certainly have recognized him. The same afternoon the local officials gathered at the spot. Although all were agreed that the man must have lain in the peat for more than a hundred years the order was given for his reinterment. So yet another bog body was lost to scientific study, like so many others before and since. In spite of this, however, important observations were made. We are told that the worked stick, which had incisions at both ends and was of fir, lay with a birch branch in cross-formation over the dead man's back, and also that the man lay in a sinkage or depression, probably an ancient peat-cutting.

The noteworthy feature of sticks over the dead body, in this case in cross-formation, is known from a long series of similar finds varying from a single stick to several lying obliquely or in a double cross formation, while other bog bodies are covered with small branches or twigs or single stones. This probably indicates the wish to pin the dead man firmly into the bog. At any rate it tells us that the person concerned did not end up in the bog by accident but was brought there by other human beings.

The woman from Haraldskjaer was even more firmly fastened in the bog, and this was also the case in a discovery made in 1790 at Bunsok, in southern Ditmarsh. While peat-cutting on 17 May of that year workmen came upon vertical birch-wood poles, three at the head and three at the feet of a bog body. These groups of vertical poles were each strengthened by three parallel horizontal sticks, and in addition poles were driven in at the sides, so that the dead person, whose sex could not be established, seemed to be enclosed in a sort of cage. The body was freed from this cage and taken to the mortuary of the military establishment at Albersdorf, where it was examined by the district medical officer. The hair on the head was red-brown and four to six inches long. No trace of any clothing was found, but a skilfully plaited band about two feet long lay at the neck. It might have been used for the hanging or strangulation of the dead person, or it might have been to blindfold him, as in one of the cases that we will be describing later.

A doubled-up female body with long blonde hair and well defined features, found in 1903 in Hingst Fen, near Kreepen, Hanover, provides another instance of a body pinned down

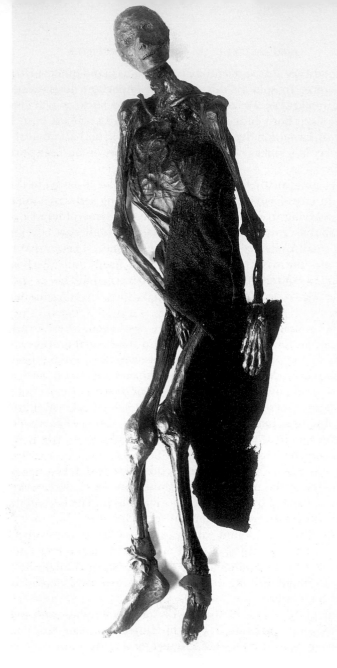

35 The bog man from Rendswühren

with unusual thoroughness. No clothing was found but there were an iron ring and two hoops made of osiers, together with two oak palings. These seem to have held the woman's arm and knees. In addition three stones each weighing about twenty-five pounds lay at her sides.

As in Denmark, the bog bodies were generally deposited naked; and clothing, when present, was arranged in a distinctive manner. A case illustrating this was a find made in June 1871 at Rendswühren Fen in the neighbourhood of Kiel. The find was investigated by Johanna Mestorf, who was Curator of the Kiel Museum at the time and in 1898 became the first German woman to be honoured with the title of Professor. An exceptionally well-preserved man lay at an angle in the bog, face downwards. He was naked except for the left leg, on which lay a piece of leather, with the pelt facing inwards, bound with leather thongs in a sort of cross-gartering. Clothing, however, consisting of a large rectangular woollen cloth and a cape made of pieces of skin sewn together, covered the man's head, which had a triangular hole in the forehead as though from a powerful blow.

This well-preserved human body naturally aroused much interest and before being despatched to Kiel it was exhibited on a farm cart in a nearby barn. During this period visitors helped themselves lavishly to souvenirs both from the body itself and from the clothing. The dead man became the first bog man to be photographed—being stood up on the tips of his toes for the purpose. Preservation of the body was carried out by smoking, for other methods of conservation were not then envisaged.

The Rendswühren man can now be seen in the Schloss Gottorp Museum in Schleswig, along with other bog finds from the district. Amongst these is the man from Damendorf, in the Eckernförde district, who lay naked under a cloak with other garments at his feet. Only his skin, hair and nails are preserved. The rest of him has completely disappeared as if by magic. A split nearly an inch long in the region of the heart may indicate how he was killed.

36 The bog man from Rendswühren

37 Only the skin, leather belt and shoes of the Damendorf man survived

Two bodies together, a man's and a woman's, were recovered at the end of June 1904 at Werdingerveen in the province of Drenthe, in Holland. They lay, naked and on their backs, rather more than eighteen inches down at the junction between the grey and the red peat. The woman rested on the man's outstretched right arm. Only his skin was preserved. He was five feet ten inches tall and in the region of the heart there was something that looked like a wound. The woman's hair was long and very fine and a shiny brown in colour, as was her skin. This discovery is preserved in the Museum at Assen.

Whether the bodies of a young woman and a man found in separate graves in Domland Fen, south of Eckernförde in Schleswig, were both deposited at the same time and should be related to each other, cannot be definitely established. The small cauldron-bog, on the Windeby estate, in which they were found, is barely an acre and a quarter in extent. It was decided in 1952 to exploit the whole of this bog for peat, using modern machinery. Happily it was decided that all the peat should be shovelled on to the conveyor belt by hand, and so the peat-workers had the chance to observe anything that might emerge from the bog.

At the end of May one of the workmen caught sight of a long bone in the bog and immediately shouted: 'Look out, here comes a stag's bone.' The next moment the engine and the conveyor-belt came to a stop—very luckily, because it was no animal bone but the lower leg of a bog body, a foot and a hand of which had already landed on the conveyor belt. The contractor very sensibly stopped work at the spot, moved his machinery elsewhere, and sent word to the County Museum of Schleswig-Holstein at Schloss Gottorp. There a state of emergency was immediately declared, for this was their first chance of studying a bog man *in situ*.

Karl Schlabow, one of the curators, and his assistants were soon at the spot. The police had already arrived, called in because some of the peat-cutters thought the body might represent a case of murder in the not too distant past. A hut

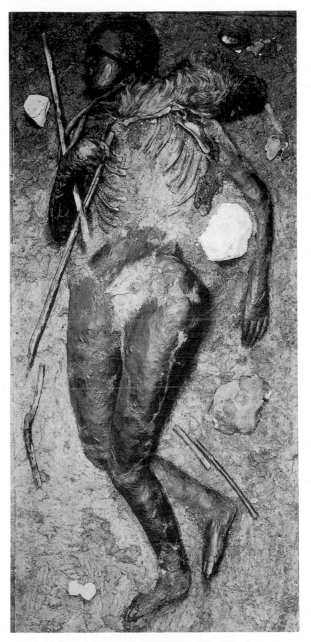

38 The young girl from the Windeby bog

encampment in which many foreign workers were housed had been set up in 1945–7 only a hundred yards away, and a number of murders had occurred in the district at that time. The expert, however, was soon able to reassure the police and to say that the body had been there for many centuries. Schlabow then took responsibility for the examination of the body on the spot and later in the museum laboratory.

Investigation quickly revealed that the body lay in an old peat-cutting. This showed as a light-coloured surface of rush-peat, five feet by seven feet in extent, surrounded by dark wood-peat going back to a very remote period. The old peat-cutting was carefully excavated layer by layer. At a depth of four feet four inches a birch-branch appeared and an inch below that a well preserved right hand, followed by the wrist, forearm and upper arm. Lowest of all, right on the bottom of the old cutting, was the head, bent sharply back and resting on the right ear. A band of cloth could be seen running from the back of the neck and passing over the face like a sling. Final examination was carried out at Schloss Gottorp, to which the body, cut out in a block of peat, was transported in a modern motor-hearse.

The body proved to be that of a young girl. She lay on her back, her head twisted to one side, the left arm outstretched. Between it and her hip was a large block of stone. The right arm was bent in against the chest, as if defensively, while the legs were lightly drawn up, the left over the right. The head, with its delicate face, and the hands, were preserved best; the chest had completely disintegrated and the ribs were visible. The lower abdomen had also gone. The hair, reddish from the effects of the bog acids but originally light blond, was of an exceptional fineness but had been shaved off with a razor on the left side of the head. Here it was less than a tenth of an inch long. On the right side of the head, in contrast, it was cut to a length of an inch and three quarters to two inches. The skin, where present, was very well preserved. The bones, though much calcified, still retained their shape.

Radiography showed the brain clearly. It seemed so well

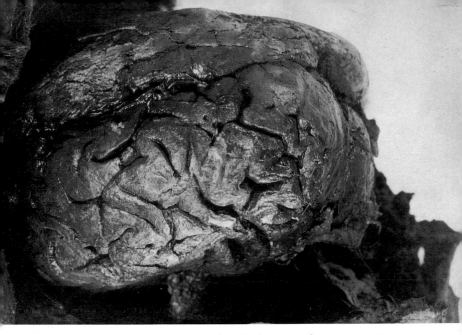

39   The Windeby girl's brain exposed

preserved that it was decided to expose it for closer examination. When the brain was removed the convolutions and folds of the surface could be clearly seen, but even after a most thorough examination it remained uncertain whether there was any difference between this brain of about two thousand years ago and the brain of contemporary man.

It will seem astonishing to many people that the brains of bog men are so well preserved, even when the bone of the skull has totally disappeared. This may be due to the presence in the brain of chloresterin, which is not soluble in water—a suggestion put forward as early as 1873, when the bog man from Rendswühren was studied.

Radiographic study of a bone of the lower leg and its growth-lines revealed that this girl of only fourteen had had an inadequate winter diet. In winter, which was cold and damp in the Early Iron Age, there must certainly have been want in many households. Pollen analysis showed that the girl had lived in the first century A.D., a date confirmed by some sherds of pottery found in and near the old cutting in which she had been deposited.

The young girl lay naked in the hole in the peat, a bandage over the eyes and a collar round the neck. The band across the eyes was drawn tight and had cut into the neck and the base of the nose. We may feel sure that it had been used to close her eyes to this world. There was no mark of strangulation on the neck, so that it had not been used for that purpose. The band is just over an inch and a quarter wide and woven from thirty-eight woollen threads in the tablet-weave technique that was used in weaving the head-gear and garments found with other bog women. It is nineteen and a half inches long, ends at both extremities in four twisted strings, and shows dark brown, bright yellow and red colour repeated in succession. It must originally have been a gay headband. The collar is a double collar of ox-hide, with red hair showing on the outside and black on the inside next to the skin. The body was subjected to a thorough examination but no trace was found of any external violence which might have caused the girl's death before she ended her days in the marsh mud. We must suppose that she was led naked out on to the bog with bandaged eyes and the collar round her neck, and drowned in the little peat pit, which must have held twenty inches of water or more. To keep the young body under, some birch branches and a big stone were laid upon her.

On 9 January 1952, only twenty days after the discovery of the girl, and a mere sixteen feet away, a man's body was found in the bog. Foot bones were sighted first in the peat-wall and word was immediately sent to the experts at Schloss Gottorp. Like the girl, the man lay in an old peat excavation, which showed up as a light-coloured patch some eight by five feet in area. The body was approached by scraping away the peat from above. At three and a quarter feet down there appeared a round piece of wood as thick as an arm, and there followed almost at once several others, making eight in all,

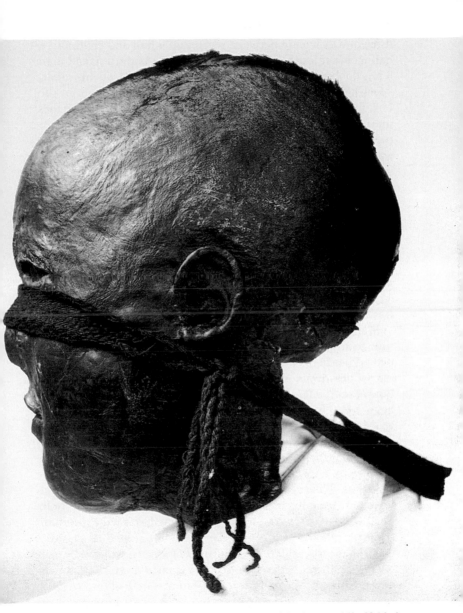

40 The Windeby girl and the band with which she was blindfolded

three of which were between seven and a half and eight and a half inches thick. Under these was the bog body, a naked man lying on his back with arms bent and crossed on his chest, knees lightly bent and feet resting right on the bottom of the bog. He was held down as though in a vice by forked branches sharpened and driven into the layer beneath the peat. Across the neck lay a flexible finger-thick hazel bough with which he was probably strangled, so that probably he was not drowned in the bog as the young girl had been.

Study of the man in the museum laboratory at Schloss Gottorp showed that the pit had been so permeated by water that the bones were completely decalcified and had disappeared. Only the man's skin and the hair of the head were preserved. The hair was from four-fifths of an inch to one inch in length and was of a striking dark colour although sprinkled with lighter hairs which had perhaps been grey. This and the large size of the pores of the skin seems to show that the man was middle-aged, or at least not very young.

Many other discoveries of bog people have been made from time to time in this same region of Eckernförde; for example, two bodies in Seemoor, near Damendorf, and two more, some four miles away, in Ruchmoor. In these same bogs many typical sacrificial objects, from different periods of antiquity, have been found. A quite outstanding find was made on 28 May 1948, in Kohlmoor, south-east of Osterby and less than two miles from Seemoor. Two men cutting peat at a depth of rather over two feet below the present-day surface came upon a human head wrapped up in a sewn cape of roe-deer skin. They realized at once the interest of their find and searched carefully in the peat already dug, and in the hole from which the head had been extracted, for other human remains, but with no result. There is thus reason to suppose that the head was deposited in the bog on its own.

Investigation in the Gottorp Museum, where the head is now exhibited, showed that it was that of a man of fifty to sixty years of age. It had been struck off by a sharp implement or weapon which had cut the second cervical vertebra in two.

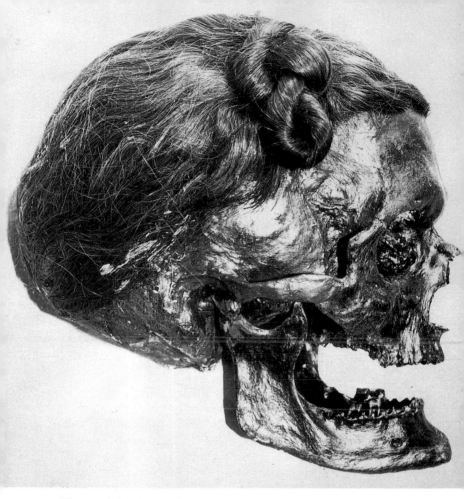

41　The man's head from Osterby, with hair tied in a 'Swabian knot'

The marks were still visible on the bone. The head was fractured on the left side, and only a small amount of skin and the hair survived. The hair is now reddish but had originally been a blond colour, not particularly light, and sprinkled with grey. It was parted at the back and was eleven inches long. It was gathered at the right side into a skilfully contrived knot, needing neither pin nor band to hold it. The hair of the neck was cut short.

Such hair-knots are known from the works of Roman sculptors in both the Rhine and the Danube regions and they are also described by Tacitus, whose treatise on the Germans was written, as we have mentioned, at the very period of the bog bodies, namely at the end of the first century A.D. Tacitus says that it is particularly the men of the Swabian tribe who wear these knots and that they are called Swabian knots for this reason. The Danish bog man from Elling has hair gathered on the left side of his head in a plait which was no doubt originally tied in such a knot. In any case, it is an important fact that the Osterby find supports Tacitus' account of the Germani in one particular, for this same account offers us a key to many of the riddles set by the bog people.

V How They Lived

On a hilly range near the village of Little Binderup stand the two splendid 'Bear Hills'. They are a landmark for the Borre Fen, where three of the Iron Age people we have already described, two women and a man, met their ends in ancient peat-workings. From these twin mounds, funeral monuments raised three millennia ago by the Bronze Age aristocracy, one overlooks great tracts of the distinctive Himmerland landscape —a landscape that has kept its ancient aspect to a considerable degree, and yielded such rich discoveries from every period of antiquity.

The great Borre Fen stretches like a golden-brown plain north and north-west to the point where the high land of Gundestrup rises to the blue sky. To the east lies the village of Kongens Thisted, with its Viking-period runic stone, and the great dark forest of Rold. In the south the horizon is formed by the imposing hill-range of Hverrestrup, with its line of Bronze Age tumuli and its slopes covered with a luxuriant ancient Danish woodland of stunted oak, aspen and bracken.

From the Bear Hills we can see the land around us open and green, sprinkled with dark heather-slopes, and with trees and vegetation clustered around the whitewashed walls of farmsteads and houses. But in the strong raking light of the setting sun these modern buildings disappear, so that in the evening we can experience the landscape once again as those people

42   The refuge-fort and Iron Age village in Borre Fen

knew it two thousand years ago, before their eyes were closed for ever in the bog. In those days, in the extreme south of the fen region, a village of a score of farms and houses stood on an island at the point where the great Borre fen passes through a narrow valley and opens out into a lesser tract of bog land. As the peat of the bog concealed the Iron Age people for two thousand years, so the grass of the island concealed their village. Now it has been excavated, and we can step from the paved village streets and follow the Iron Age people in over their thresholds.

Like most Jutland peasant houses of two thousand years ago those of the village in Borre Fen were dwellings for both men and animals. The houses are clustered together and all aligned east and west, with the winter quarters for the animals at the east end. Most of them are grouped round the village street, which begins on the mainland, on firm ground, as a paved stone built carriageway ten feet wide, and runs out across the bog on a causeway to the island. Here it winds in among the houses, interrupted only at one point by a gutter, and ends at the centre of the island as a path little more than a yard wide. The houses are all built on the same plan but vary in size. The biggest is eighty-eight feet long and twenty-three feet wide and the smallest half this length and somewhat narrower. All the houses had two lines of free-standing posts down their length to support the roof, and walls of turf and roofs of straw or heather thatch. They made warm, snug dwellings for the Iron Age folk and their beasts in the long dark winters, when the peat blocks glowed brightly on the hearth and the cows munched hay from the loft above their stalls.

One of the houses was burnt down while the village was inhabited and has lain there ever since, covered with ashes, just as it was when the fire burnt out, two thousand years ago. Such an undisturbed burnt dwelling brings us into immediate contact with the daily life of the Iron Age people; and in the course of years many such burnt houses have been uncovered in the Jutland peninsula.

The burnt house in the Borre Fen village is not a big one. It measures forty-two feet by nineteen feet six inches. Around the whole perimeter, except at the west end, heavy stones laid side by side marked out the foundations. Inside these was flat paving, probably a foundation for benches or plank beds. In the centre of the floor, towards the west, lay the clay platform of the hearth, burnt red, and engraved with two concentric circles, one running near its edge and the other a little more than two inches further in; perhaps marking the permitted limit of the fire in the inflammable building. In the middle of the two long sides, the north and south walls, threshold stones lay opposite each other, with carbonized wood from the doors. Perhaps it was this arrangement that led to the burning down of the house. The smoke from the open hearth found its way out through a louvre or hole in the gable. A cross-draught probably carried a spark up into the very inflammable rush- and heather-covered roof, and so the whole house was burnt down.

Right at the west end of the house the contents of the 'kitchen', burnt red by the fire, lay practically undisturbed. Around a large quern-stone—a saddle-quern, with an almost completely hollowed-out bed and a separate pounder or grinder—on which the women of the house had ground corn and barley, lay many pottery vessels; large ones for storing the winter's supplies and also smaller dishes and drinking vessels. A dish with a perforated base had served as a strainer or sieve, perhaps for cheese-making. The women from the bog with their rough and work-worn hands, may have ground corn for their bread on this quern; it could even have been used to prepare the last meal of the Borre Fen bog man. The quern remains today in its original position in the house, for the village has been preserved as an ancient monument, and is accessible to visitors. By the side of the quern lay a cake of burnt clay filled with pellets and stumps of straw, about as big as a good-sized shrove-tide pancake and on its upper surface a cross was inscribed. It is perhaps the earliest known 'scrap-cake'. In Denmark many of us remember 'scrap-cakes' from

43　Iron Age long-house in Borre Fen, in the course of excavation

our childhood. When bread or cakes were mixed on a dish or in moulds the last remnants of dough were scraped up and from them a special cake was made, the 'scrap-cake', the best cake the children were ever given. In former days the scrap-cake used to be put out for the goblins. The cake found in the Iron Age house was certainly intended for these or similar powers that protected the house and its animal and human inmates against the powers of evil. Elsewhere in the house a clay disc was found with the finger prints of a small girl all over the upper surface. It was perhaps a piece of potters clay left over from the last occasion when pots were made.

The old farmsteads were bad fire-risks. We know of instances where a whole village was burnt down at one time. This happened to a small Iron Age village at Fjande near Nissum fjord in West Jutland. Catastrophe struck in the first century A.D.: the complete village, eight homesteads in all, was burnt down simultaneously; for the houses lay so close together—they were only separated by narrow alleys—that the fire leaped from roof to roof. After the fire the village was built afresh, and this time a hole was dug in one of the burnt houses and in it an iron axe was set with the cutting-edge turned upwards. It is quite likely that the fire was started by lightning, and the iron axe was buried with its edge pointing at the sky to ward off a similar fate for the new village. 'Prophylactic magic', as the excavator of the village, Professor Gudmund Hatt, writes: 'a weapon turned against the weapon of the thunder, a cutting edge against a cutting edge'. And the little village, be it noted, was not burnt again.

While the inhabitants of the Borre Fen village were ordinary Jutland peasants, tillers of the land, with barley and corn as their most common grains, and cows and sheep as their normal livestock, the Iron Age inhabitants of Fjande were also fisherfolk, as most of the villagers along the west coast of Jutland have been from remote times down to our own day. The evidence for this was not merely the presence of fish-bones in the occupation layers but also of net-sinkers in all the houses. One pile of net-weights, seventeen in number, of a type that has remained in use up and down the west coast of Jutland from that day to this, indicates a fishing-net sixty-five feet long.

The village on the island in Borre Fen, which was occupied in the first century B.C., had been raised upon older foundations dating from an earlier phase of the Celtic Iron Age. In this period the inhabitants of the island had constructed a veritable fortress, a town of refuge, in which the occupants of the neighbouring villages and their cattle could seek shelter in times of unrest.

The design was carefully thought out and skilfully executed. A deep defensive ditch was dug round the whole island and the earth was thrown up on the inside to form a rampart. The surface of the fen around the island was dug away so that a swamp was created. Through this swamp the only entry was across a paved ford, hidden beneath the surface of the water, and flanked by deep ditches, so that it could only be safely negotiated by those who knew it intimately. The refuge-fort in Borre Fen perhaps reflects the troubled period in the Early Iron Age when the Cimbri and the Teutones were leaving their homeland in Jutland and moving south—where they came near to toppling the great Roman Empire in its first days of prosperity.

That there were class distinctions in Danish society in the Early Iron Age, and that we only know the dwellings of one class, the long houses of the peasantry, is not to be disputed. The existence of these distinctions stands out clearly from the corpus of Iron Age finds, and particularly from the grave-goods of the centuries following the birth of Christ, in which an increasingly sharp division between the social classes becomes steadily apparent.

Even if many of the Early Iron Age men who have come to light in bogs can be reckoned to have belonged to the peasantry, this need not be so of them all. Some may have belonged to the priesthood, whose leading figures may have exercised secular power in greater or lesser tribal areas as chiefs or minor kings. As for the peasants, the examination of

44   Contents of a Jutland Iron Age man's purse.
From the Ginderup village site

the young girl from Domland Fen at Windeby in Schleswig showed that she could suffer from deficiencies in diet over the winter months, and this deficiency must have been characteristic of the north of Jutland no less than the south. Yet as many discoveries indicate, the peasants were not poor.

Thus in an Iron Age house at Ginderup in Thy, North-West Jutland, a hoard of current Roman coins was found. In such a context the find is unique and calls for special explanation. It comprised a gold coin with the stern head of Nero on the obverse, and on the reverse Jupiter Custos enthroned, and twenty-four silver coins, sixteen of which are Republican denarii and the rest coins of the first Emperors. The oldest of the coins, struck between 124 and 102 B.C., bears on one face the representation of the Goddess Roma and on the other that of the Goddess Freedom in a *quadriga*.* The latest has a portrait of Vespasian and was struck in A.D. 74. The treasure, buried in a hole dug beside the hearth, lay in a heap, as though the coins had all been contained in a purse. The owner must have hidden the hoard and not revealed its hiding place before his death.

The orientation and arrangement of the house indicate that its owner was in some way exceptional.

It was a small house, twenty-three feet by thirteen feet, and similar to the other houses of the village in its construction. It did not, however, like these, run east and west, but north and south. The hearth lay on a clay platform at the south end and the kitchen utensils on a sanded floor at the north end. The owner of the coins may have been a native of Thy who had served as a legionary in the Roman army and perhaps held rank as an officer and spoke Latin. Subsequently he had returned to his native village with his savings, and built himself a house at right-angles to the traditional alignment. The hoard as a whole shows that this occurred about A.D. 100, at just the time when Tacitus was writing his book about the Germani.

Decorated hearths in several Early Iron Age houses in Jut-

* A *quadriga* is a chariot drawn by a team of four horses.

land suggest that one of the local inhabitants had had first-hand experience of Roman mosaics, having perhaps served the Romans as a mercenary or taken part in one of those trading expeditions on which the products of Roman industry, such as bronze and glass vessels, were exchanged with furs, slaves and amber. These hearths are often found in houses which already have ordinary hearths for baking and cooking. They consist of a smooth clay floor marked off with incised lines into rectangular frames surrounding areas carrying incised or stamped designs, reminiscent of Roman mosaic pavements. It is thus possible that those who made them, perhaps for a special purpose, such as the burning of the produce of the soil as an offering, had visited Roman houses with mosaic floors.

One or two of the houses in the village at Ginderup shed some light for us on how the clothing found with the dead in the bogs was manufactured. In one, of about A.D. 200, a pile of loom-weights of baked clay was found to the right of the entrance, between two of the posts supporting the roof. The pile of weights lay between two holes in the sand floor, which, with the weights, indicate that at this point stood a vertical loom of the kind familiar to us from representations on Greek vases of the middle of the first millennium B.C. On such a loom all the examples of textiles that we know from the bogs could have been woven; and that accounts for practically all we have of Iron Age clothing. To the evidence of the actual examples of garments from the bogs we can only add that of the small fragments of cloth found in graves, and what may be seen in contemporary Roman depictions of natives of the north taken as prisoners. The actual garments that have been found agree closely with those depicted in the Roman sculptures. This in turn reinforces the value of the sculptures as a source of information about the Germanic peoples.

These Iron Age garments of the north are themselves unique. Through them one comes into direct contact with the distinctive two-thousand-year-old textile art of the Iron Age, with the character and pattern of the cloth, and with weaving techniques. Moreover, they are 'alive' with wear and marks of use in the years before they accompanied their owners into the bog. Dr Margrethe Hald, the expert who has spent a lifetime in the study of the garments of antiquity, and to whom we chiefly owe our knowledge of them, has been able with her own hands to sort out the original folds and shape of the garments when they were in use. They have thus preserved for us something which even the best of the contemporary works of art cannot convey.

The most splendid of them all are two woman's outfits from Huldre Fen, in Djursland (see pp. 79, 80). They probably date from the earliest phase of the Iron Age and even if they can only be dated rather precariously, on the evidence of the horn comb found in the pocket of one of them, it is nevertheless likely that similar costume was worn during the greater part of the Early Iron Age. The garments from Huldre Fen are from two different finds, two skin capes, a woven scarf and a skirt being found with the women discovered in 1879. The skirt was gathered slightly at one side in the actual weaving process, at the exact point where there are now remains of leather laces, so that its ultimate function as a skirt was in mind even as the cloth was being woven. A neat squared pattern was obtained by the alternation of two yarns of different colour: two natural wool colours, a golden brown and a very dark brown, being used. Plate 45 shows how this skirt might have been worn with one of the capes. Covering for the upper part of the body is admittedly lacking, but the shawl which was found at the woman's neck, with a birdbone pin as a fastening, may have served this purpose.

The other outfit from Huldre Fen holds a leading place amongst ancient costumes both for its shape and its technique. It was found a little after the discovery of the woman whose clothing has just been described, but in almost the same spot. It consists of a single tubular piece of cloth, five feet seven inches in length and nine feet in circumference, and is like a sack open at both ends. It is woven in a special way known as circular weaving. A complete dress, not a skirt, this type of

45　Clothing from Huldre Fen

garment was arranged on the shoulders into a pretty, sleeve-less gown with numerous folds. It is very similar to what was worn by Greek women as seen in vase painting of the fifth century B.C. (that is to say, contemporary with the Huldre Fen outfits)—a dress called the *peplos* and thought to have originated with the Dorians. As Plate 45 shows, the garment is folded outwards over the shoulders into an attractive flap or hood. This is practical too, since the fold can be turned up over the head and can cover the face in cold or bad weather. A very similar garment is worn by Germanic women in the reliefs on the columns of Trajan and Marcus Aurelius in Rome, representations corresponding in date with the Roman Iron Age in Denmark. Evidence that this particular type of costume was worn through the whole of the early Iron Age is to be found in the ornamental brooches which occur in pairs amongst the grave furniture of the period, and by means of which the garment was gathered at the shoulders.

A cap also formed part of a woman's attire. The only completely preserved example is the one from the bog in the forest of Arden (Plate 27). It is of fine yellowish-brown woollen yarn and made in the delicate technique known as 'sprung', a charming piece of feminine handicraft and very becoming over hair coiled into a crown, as worn by the girl from the Arden bog.

Male dress is far less well represented in the bog finds; and what there is seems to give an incomplete picture of it, for it consists of practically nothing but skin shoulder-capes which could only have covered a very small area of the upper body. This agrees with the account of the Germani given by Julius Caesar, who encountered them in his Gallic wars in the middle of the first century B.C. Caesar says that they wore a short garment of skin but were otherwise naked. Germanic captives are so represented in Roman reliefs. Tacitus, too, says of the Germani that the universal dress amongst them is a cape fastened by a brooch (the safety-pin of the time) or for those who lacked a brooch, by a thorn, and further that they would spend the whole day by the hearth or fire wearing no other

46 Chained and naked northerners wearing short skin capes

garment. He adds, however, that the more prosperous wore a fitted garment which sat tightly on every limb—the costume, that is, worn by the men depicted on the Gunderstrup cauldron.

Tacitus also recounts that the spear-carrying Germanic infantry in battle were either naked or wore a short cape. There is thus a marked agreement between the contemporary literary sources and the bog finds. None the less this mode of dress comes as a surprise when one compares it with that of the Bronze Age—long coat, cape and cap—and when one recalls that the weather at this period, the beginning of the Iron Age, was colder and wetter than in the preceding period.

The bogs have contributed other items to male costume besides the skin capes, which have been sometimes found in pairs, an inner worn with the hair inwards and an outer with the hair outwards. As we have seen, several bog finds have produced caps or bonnets of skin; others have yielded leggings, which were bound to the calves with woollen strings. Leggings of this sort were found with a man's body in Daugbjerg Fen in 1944. The find also included a skin coat similar in cut to the woven coats of the Bronze Age. But woven cloths with fringes, having no special cut, have also been found with bog men and these could very well have been worn as outer coats, as un-shaped lengths of cloth are worn amongst many primitive peoples.

Thus in the main the finds tell us that male costume in the Early Iron Age consisted of cap, cape, coat, leggings and shoes. Only towards the end of the period, and then in the great deposits of war-gear, do trousers and sleeved shirts or tunics appear. It is not impossible, however, that these may have been brought into use earlier but failed to register amongst the bog-finds. They could, for example, have been made of linen and not have survived for this reason. The weaving of linen was already known in the late Bronze Age, the plant used being the nettle. Flax was also known. This last, primarily looked upon as a food plant because of its grain, was probably also used for making textiles—but linen cloth disintegrates very easily in bogs. When we look at the Tollund man 'lying asleep', we can readily visualize him clad in a tunic belted at the waist, and perhaps in trousers. Something of the sort is called for to provide a natural explanation for his belt. Germanic warriors are furthermore shown on the column of Marcus Aurelius in Rome wearing a variety of garments. Some wear cape, shirt and trousers, others are trousered with sleeveless tunic or wear trousers and shirt without a cape. These depictions of Germani on the column are of the end of the second century B.C. and so of the Tollund man's period.

Only in one or two cases do the dead in the bogs have with them any personal possessions, other than clothing. An instance was the woman from Huldre Fen who had a horn comb in a small pocket in one of her skin capes. Another was the young girl from Corselitze who wore a brooch and a string of beads. However, we know the *personalia* of both men and women from other discoveries. In the long span of time— eight centuries—covered by the Early Iron Age, however, clothing and other items underwent many changes, and we can only give a limited number of examples. Moreover, within the big areas characterized by this ancient Danish culture there were naturally many districts in which ornaments and toilet articles took on a local stamp.

In the four centuries B.C. known as the Celtic Iron Age, because in it the great Celtic kingdoms of Central and Western Europe strongly influenced the northern lands, the dead were burnt on a pyre and took only little in the way of grave-goods with them. Consequently our knowledge of *personalia* in this period is relatively meagre. Bronze and iron pins of different sorts, provided with a catch-plate on the foot, so that they would not fall out of the cloth they were designed to fasten, are common in the earlier graves. Bowed brooches, working on the principle of the modern safety-pin, are also known from these graves, but they do not become common until the end of the Celtic Iron Age. Iron shears and crescent-shaped razors, used to trim the hair and beard, are also found

47 Romans forcing Germans to decapitate each other. Scene from
the Column of Marcus Aurelius in Rome, about A.D. 193

in the graves. The bog bodies that have been found seem to show that men went clean-shaven and women in many cases wore bobbed or short cropped hair. Belt-hooks, flat belt-buckles and slides also often occur in the graves, indicating that belts were used, either to hold up trousers or as a waist-belt for tunics, which were worn by men and women alike.

A special class of objects—rings—were buried in the ground or thrown into bogs as offerings to the gods of fertility and good fortune. These were neck-rings, wristlets or ankle-rings of bronze, and sometimes of gold. They are often found in pairs. The greatest discovery of this sort is that from Smederup in East Jutland. It consists of about 350 rings made of thin bronze wire, together with a number of belt-buckles. The whole was deposited in a wooden well which had been set in a small hole dug into the bog.

The second half of the Iron Age, which covers the centuries following the birth of Christ, has proved much more prolific in discoveries of ornaments and objects for personal use, for in this period a change took place from cremation to inhumation, which rapidly became the sole funerary rite.

These centuries are known in Scandinavia as the Roman Iron Age, since in this period (as already noted) the north was much influenced by the Romans who were steadily enlarging their world empire in this direction, as well as elsewhere. This process brought them into direct contact with the Germanic peoples, who were written about by Roman historians and depicted by Roman artists. In the Roman Iron Age, and especially in East Jutland and the islands, there existed a ruling class who maintained profitable connections with the Roman Empire and probably had personal contacts with high officials of the Empire, both civil and military.

The richest graves of this period contain magnificent sets of drinking vessels and larger containers, not only of bronze and glass but also of silver, which were the work of craftsmen of the first rank. These sumptuous pieces may have reached the north as presents to northern notabilities. We need only refer, for this period, to the chieftain's grave at Hoby on the island

48 Part of a Lolland Iron Age chieftain's grave furniture, of Roman silver and bronze. From the burial-site at Hoby

of Lolland, in which the dead chief lay surrounded by rich equipment. On a bronze dish near the dead man's head stood two exquisite silver goblets with scenes from Greek legend and signed by Greek craftsmen working for Roman patrons. In one of the wine-goblets was a small silver cup with a handle terminating in an animal's head. To the right of the dead man's head stood a group of Roman bronze vessels—a dish, a wine-jug or ewer, a saucepan and a situla or bucket for wine —and three pottery bowls and two drinking horns of native manufacture. There were also in the grave five bow-brooches, two gold rings, a knife and a bone pin. As provision for his journey to the land of the dead, the chieftain was given two legs of pork and some joints of lamb.

A woman's grave from the same district, found at Jelling, revealed comparable wealth. Her hair-pins, necklets, costume jewellery and finger-rings were of gold and silver. Above her head lay her toilet-box with bronze lock and key-plate, and inside this were a bone comb and pin and a bronze knife and scissors. The grave also contained two finely cut and ground glass vessels of Roman origin, two native drinking-horns, a large bronze cauldron and a bronze ladle which matched a strainer held in her right hand. In addition to beer, which the cauldron had contained, this lady of standing was provided with steaks of pork and beef as food for her journey.

The grave-furniture of the Jutland peasant was more modest, but he too was equipped so that he might accomplish the journey to the next world. He did not, like the more distinguished, lie alone, or with one or two others, in a small burial-place, but along with all his fellow villagers—men, women and children—numbering perhaps several hundreds, in one place. But even the peasant lay in the grave at table, after the fashion of a Roman nobleman. It was spread in front of him with drinking vessels, bowls and dishes of native pottery. He too had cuts of pork, beef and mutton placed by his side. With them a carving-knife was placed ready. Sometimes his hand still held the foot of a drinking-cup.

To the evidence for the way of life of the Iron Age people

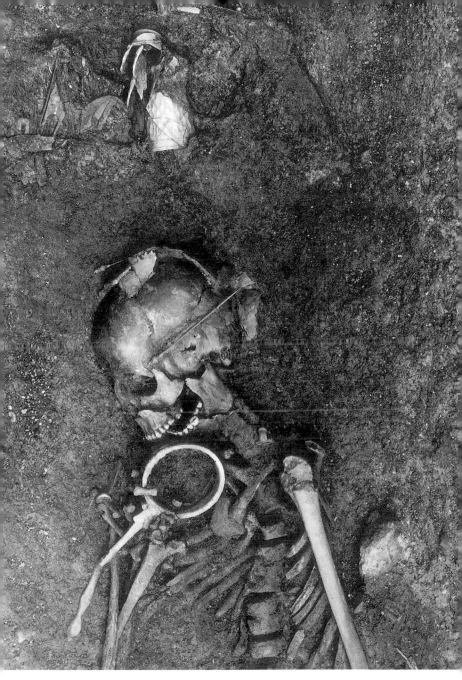

49 Woman of rank with Roman wine-ladle, glass goblet and ornaments

50   An Iron Age peasant, with his furniture of pottery vessels
containing food. From the Lisbjerg Iron Age cemetery

which discoveries on native soil provide, we can add the testimony of contemporary classical writers. They cannot of course have all been equally well informed and they very seldom speak of the people of the north. It is their more southerly relatives of the same stock that are described, who no doubt closely resembled them in customs and manners. One can also recognize in the authors' descriptions, especially those of Cornelius Tacitus, an attempt to hold up the simple life and pure customs of the Germani in the day of the Tollund and Grauballe men as an example to the debauched Romans.

The first significant known contact between the southern peoples and the races of the north is the irruption of the Cimbri and Teutones into central and West Europe in the years 115–101 B.C. They won several victories over the Romans but were then struck down by the Roman general Marius, who first defeated them at Aix-en-Provence in 102 B.C., when he took King Theudobod prisoner, and finally defeated the Cimbri, on 1 July, 101 B.C., at Vercelli, in North Italy. These peoples are supposed to have come ultimately from Jutland, the Cimbri from Himmerland and the Teutones from Thy, but there is no compelling evidence for this. However, the theory receives support from the Greek geographer Ptolemy, who lived in Alexandria in the second century B.C. His *Geography* was illustrated with twenty-seven maps. In one of these he called Jutland the Cimbric peninsula and places the Cimbri in the most northerly part of it.

The men in the Cimbrian army are described as tall in build with blue eyes and fair hair, open in character, and credulous, so that they are easily taken in; but ferocious and fearless in battle. It is said of their crossing of the Alps that they tobogganed down the snow-slopes on their shields, giving out ear-splitting yells, and that they waded out into mountain torrents in closed ranks in order to dam the water up against their chests.

The Spanish early Christian patristic writer, Paul Orosius, writing in the fifth century A.D., describes their frenzy after their victory over the Romans at Orange. 'Their (the

Romans') clothes were torn to pieces and thrown away, gold and silver were thrown into the river, armour was hacked into pieces, horse trappings were broken up and the horses themselves drowned in the swirling waters of the river. In short, there was no more booty for the victors than pity for the vanquished.' Their women showed much the same characteristics, and grey-haired priestesses carried out human sacrifices to the gods. Caesar, too, praises the incredible bravery of the Germani in battle and their warlike nature, insisting at the same time on their savagery and perfidy; one cannot blame him when one thinks of all the trouble they caused him.

The most detailed description is that of Tacitus in his book on the Germani (the *Germania*). The Germani were said to be the peoples east of the Rhine and to the north, in distinction from the Celts who lived to the west of the Rhine. Tacitus says that the Germani did not intermarry with other peoples, and that consequently most of them are of similar appearance —rough or wild in aspect, with blue eyes and red hair, tall in stature, and with a natural skill in attack. They do not stand up well to heat and thirst, but their climate and soil has compensated by inuring them to cold and hunger. They are brave in battle and seek to die with their lord, whom they may outlive only with shame. In peace time they have no higher authority, for it is the chieftain who enforces the law amongst them. Their friendliness and hospitality knows no bounds. They are generous and friendly amongst themselves and to their guests. They sleep late in the morning and take equal pleasure in feasting and in work. They get drunk on home-brewed beer and play at dice without bothering whether they win or lose. They even gamble with their own persons in the last resort and give themselves voluntarily into slavery.

In morals they set an example which, Tacitus says, might well be followed. They take marriage very seriously and almost alone amongst barbarians they content themselves with one woman. From this rule certain men are exempted who are particularly well qualified to be sons-in-law because of their high standing; but polygamy is not sought for sensual pleasure. The man brings the dowry to the marriage, and it is not a dowry intended to satisfy feminine vanity, but may consist of oxen, a fully equipped and appointed horse, a shield, spear and sword. Such are the gifts which a bride receives and she herself gives her man weapons. Only after this exchange can the instinct of love have its way, which Tacitus gives as a reason for the preservation of the virility of the Germani. Nor do the young women show any haste, so that youthful strength and fine physique is equally preserved amongst women. For this we can cite the corroboration of Caesar who says that any man of the Germani who has relations with a woman before her twentieth year is considered to have acted very shamefully.

There are various sources of information about the religion of the Germani. Thus Caesar says that they only worship the gods of nature, the sun, the moon and fire, while Tacitus, writing one and a half centuries later, names three principal gods, the chief of them Mercury, to whom on special days human sacrifice was made, and Hercules and Mars, who the Germani sought to win over with sacrifice of animals. Under their Roman names one can recognize the leading Germanic gods, Odin, Thor and Tyr. Human sacrifice is associated both with Mercury and with a female deity Nerthus (who was worshipped chiefly by a string of small Germanic tribes in the north west) in terms—applying also to penalties for certain crimes—which call to mind the bog people and explain why it was that many ended their days in the grip of the peat.

VI When Death Came

Death is the inescapable lot of man, and it comes in many guises. Among the Iron Age people from the peat bogs we have seen the signs of death in its grimmest forms. Young and old, men and women, met their ends by decapitation, strangulation, cutting of the throat, hanging and drowning. Very probably they suffered torture, mutilation and dismemberment before they died. Yet these are the ones the bogs have preserved as individuals down to our own day, while all their relatives and contemporaries from the eight centuries of the Iron Age have totally vanished or at the most only survive as skeletons in their graves.

We cannot view as one uniform phenomenon the many bog people from this long span of time, for during it great changes came about in religious beliefs and ideas of law, and both must be borne in mind if we are to find an explanation of these extraordinary discoveries. How great the changes were may be judged, amongst other things, from the general shift in burial rite, from cremation to inhumation, already briefly mentioned.

In the first half of the age of the bog people cremation was supreme. The dead were burnt on a pyre. At first their bones were carefully picked out of the ashes and buried in a variety of ways; sometimes, in burial urns or wrapped in cloth, they were buried in a mound of an older period; sometimes they were buried under very low mounds in extensive gravefields.

In Jutland many hundreds of such mounds occur together. At other times the bones were deposited in flat ground. Grave-goods were few—a brooch, an ornament, a little scrap of metal, this last perhaps a symbolic payment for the journey to the land of the dead. Later on, remains of the pyre, on to which all the grave-goods now followed the body, were gathered up with the burnt bones for burial. Finally, by the time of the birth of Christ, the dead were once more being inhumed, with abundant provision of grave-goods. This rite lasted out the Roman era.

This great change in burial custom undoubtedly reflects a corresponding change in ideas about death. But cremation and inhumation, however radical the difference between them, were normal burial rites, and there is a great gulf between those so buried and those who ended up in the bogs.

Cremation, appearing in the north as early as the Stone Age, two thousand years before Christ, becoming supreme in the Early Bronze Age and running on through the Celtic Iron Age, is bound up with the belief that the soul is freed from the body with the help of fire, and flies to a distant land of the dead, where it is re-born. We find this explanation given in the funeral hymns of the Hindus, which tell us that fire, as the servant of God, conveys the dead to the kingdom where gods and ancestors dwell. The same belief occurs amongst the Indian tribes of the Pacific coast of America, who also practice cremation:

'Unless the body is burnt the soul will never reach the land of the dead' . . . 'In the hot smoke it rises up to the shining sun to rejoice in its warmth and light; then it flies away to the happy land in the west.'

A cremation in a mound at Alestrup, south of Borre Fen in Himmerland, suggests that the survivors, in their concern for the dead, sought to assist this celestial flight. Mixed with the bones of a young person were the burnt bones of the cut-off wings of at least six jackdaws and two crows, as well as two crows' feet. We cannot doubt the intention behind the laying of so many wings on the pyre along with the body. Twelve small and four large wings were to bear the soul to the land of the dead.

By contrast, in the era of cremation, sacrificial offerings were connected with marsh and water. Thousands of pottery vessels of this period, containing offerings of food—legs of meat, steaks of animal flesh, gruel made from corn and seed—are found deposited in bogs just as the human bodies are. They are offerings by the Iron Age peasants to ensure a good harvest or to thank the presiding deities for their help. For the upper classes the priest-chieftains deposited great treasures in the bogs—bronze and silver vessels, costly torcs, valuable weapons, and other precious things. We also find women's clothing and cut-off hair, waggons and ploughs, all deposited by peasantry or aristocracy according to their status. More important still to our understanding of the bog people is the fact that it is in bogs, and in specific localities, that the representations of the gods from this period have come to light.

In the centuries after Christ, known in Scandinavia as the Roman Iron Age—the final period of the bog people—a more materialistic conception of death becomes apparent. As we have seen, we find the Jutland peasants lying in their graves as though at a table set for a feast; with porridge and beer in pottery vessels, steaks with carving-knives beside them, and jugs and pans containing various other provisions. The upper classes are even more richly provided for, with bronze and silver vessels in addition to the native pottery. Sometimes we encounter in the graves complete services of smashed earthenware, so that we can visualize the wake being held at the site of the grave itself. The occasional deposition, after the burial, of vessels containing food suggests that the sojourn of the dead person in his earthly grave was believed to last for some time.

But people in the Roman Iron Age also believed in a kingdom where the dead, after some passage of time, resided. Gold coins found in the mouths of the dead show that it was necessary to pay for the journey there. This custom corresponds to the one in classical lands, where a coin so placed was intended to pay the tax levied by the ferryman Charon who carried the dead across the stream that separated the lands of the living and the dead. It still survives into our own day in Jutland, unwittingly and in a different form. The fishermen carry a Charon coin in one ear in the form of a small gold ring, so that in case of disaster at sea they may be sure of being able to pay for being carried across the stream to the kingdom of the dead.

Surveying the vast corpus of finds from Denmark's Early Iron Age and relating our knowledge to the numerous discoveries of bog people, it emerges clearly that the circumstances of the bog people's deposition show nothing in common with normal burial customs, but on the contrary have many of the characteristics of the sacrificial deposits. Probably, then, the bog people were offered to the same powers as the other bog finds, and belong to the gods. Were this not so, there would be no reason for them to be in the bogs, which at this time in the Early Iron Age stood out as small woods in an otherwise almost treeless landscape. This matches Tacitus' account of the Germanic divinities: 'Furthermore they do not consider it compatible with the greatness of the heavenly powers to confine their gods within four walls or to represent them in the likeness of a human face. They consecrate groves and coppices, and give the name God to that secret presence which they can see only in awe and adoration.' Naturally we must except from this interpretation those who ended their days in the bog by accident, such as those who went astray in fog or rain and were drowned, one dark autumn day. We must also except those who were murdered and hidden in bogs, away from the beaten track. Several such are known amongst the bog people; but by far the greater number of the bog people, where proper observations are recorded, bear the stamp of sacrificial offerings.

A parish register from Hermannsburg in Germany records that on St John's Day, 24 June 1450, a number of peasants and responsible people from Bönsdörp came to the parish priest, Magnus Lauenrod, at Harmsborg, and informed him that they had found a dead man in Bormswisch, stuck fast in a peat-bog up to his neck. They were wondering whether to bury him again, or what they should do. The priest, however, advised them to leave the man alone, since it was up to the elves who had lured him out into the bog to attend to him, and they would soon cover him up again so that there would be nothing to see there any more. He also pointed out that only Christians might be buried in the churchyard, and that since elves inhabited the part of the bog where the man had met his death, the devil had undoubtedly got him. As it happened, on the following day there was nothing left to be seen at the spot.

By a fatal mischance a peasant and a girl were drowned in an English bog in a snowstorm on 14 January 1675. They were found on 3 May the same year but were buried again in the bog on the instructions of the coroner. Twenty-nine years later an inquisitive peasant opened the double grave and found the two bodies quite fresh, with the skin unbroken and maintaining their original colour as at the time of death. After that the luckless couple were exhibited annually at the local fair and the surviving relatives did not succeed until 1716 in putting a stop to this macabre display.

A murder nearly six hundred years old in Halland, on the west coast of Sweden, was brought to light in 1936 by a Swedish scholar, Dr Albert Sandklef. He was on his way to the midsummer dance at the coastal resort of Varberg when an acquaintance told him that a dead man had been found in a bog. The body had already been seen by the local policeman and a doctor. A farmer of Bocksten had discovered the body in his peat-bog, where he was breaking up the soft top layer with a harrow to make peat litter. Over the years this operation had lowered the level of the bog by about two feet six inches. Whilst work was in progress, shortly before midsummer day, the harrow got caught in a piece of cloth. When this was examined more closely it was seen to enclose a human head practically black in colour but with reddish-brown hair and beard-stubble. The policeman at his visit removed a woven cape; part of a tunic; two leather straps, one of which had been on the dead man's body serving as a belt, while the other was a little way off; two dagger-sheaths with wooden handles still attached to them, though the bog-acids had eaten away the blades; two shoes, and leather pieces that had belonged to the shoes; an oak paling which had been driven through the dead man's body but had been extracted by the doctor; and lastly one of the dead man's feet, which was covered in woollen cloth. Dr Sandklef began investigating the discovery on the morning of midsummer day, in the peat-bog. When he had dug through the one-foot-deep peat straw that covered the spot he found the upper part of the dead man's body, the lower jaw, a cloth hood drawn out into a long point at the back (of the kind known as an 'ostrich hood'), various pieces of cloth and parts of two birch-wood stakes. Only the trouser-clad legs of the dead man lay approximately in their original positions. The foot that had already been removed was the only part of the body missing. Study of the body showed that the man was about thirty-five years old and six feet one inch tall, and that he had lain face downwards and fully clothed, the left hand extended at his side and the right bent in front of his chest. There were traces of a fatal blow on the left side of the head. Originally the dead man had been deposited just below the surface of the peat, which was probably scraped to one side and then raked over him again. In the course of time the overlying peat had reached a depth of nearly two feet six inches. To stop the dead man 'walking' his murderers had driven a birch stake through his back just above the buttocks and another at his side, though this last had only gone through his clothing. Finally, a stake of oak cut from a piece of building-timber had been driven through his heart, so that the ghost might not harm the murderers.

From the exceptional dress, and particularly the distinctive hood, the murder could be fixed at about the year 1360. At this time the Danish King Valdemar Atterdag was

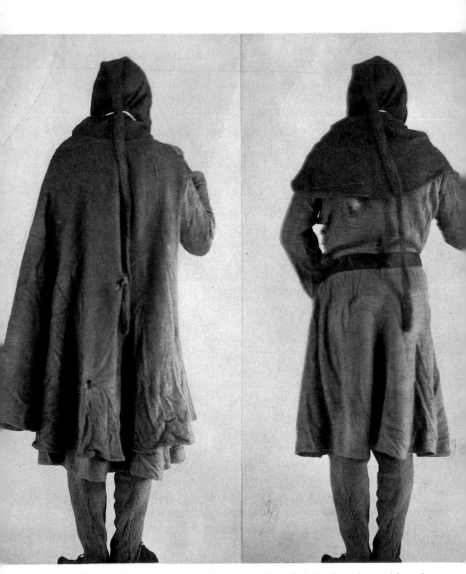

51 The Bocksten man, murdered and pinned down in a bog with stakes around the year A.D. 1360

campaigning against Halland, in the north. He took Varberg Castle in 1366. Albert Sandklef accordingly suggested that the bog man of Bocksten might have been an agent sent out to rouse the peasants of the district against their Danish King. The peasants, however, did not care to fight against their former lord, and put the agent to death. He was then hidden in the Bocksten fen; and by burying him in this spot the peasants insured themselves against his taking revenge upon them. The bog is the meeting-point of four parishes and according to old beliefs he would not be able to escape from such a spot to revenge himself on his murderers. The fact that the body was carefully and firmly pinned with wooden stakes indicates that they sought extra protection.

If in the attempt to understand these finds we look beyond the evidence provided by the bog people themselves, we are invariably brought back to the contemporary work of Tacitus on the Germani. He speaks to us directly across the gap of almost 2,000 years. Many of his sources have long since been lost, but a good deal of their content is incorporated in his narrative. Even if we cannot take everything he says as literal truth, we can be sure that his account reflects the essential facts about the subject that particularly concerns us— the deaths of the bog people. Though scholars may be correct in saying that Tacitus' book on the Germani is not an historical document so much as an unreliable record of oral tradition, nevertheless a long series of archaeological finds agrees with what he tells us. His account in general can probably be relied on, more especially as bog people occur among the south Germans, of whom Tacitus primarily wrote, in the same circumstances as they do in the north Germanic areas.

Human sacrifice in antiquity is known of from many sources. We have already referred to the Cimbri, who after victory hang their conquered enemies in trees with ropes round their necks, and human sacrifice is probably depicted on the great silver cauldron from Gundestrup (p. 171 ff., Plates 66–70). Tacitus writes of the Germanic tribe, the Semmones:

At a time laid down in the distant past all peoples that are related by blood meet through their delegations in a wood, which the prophetic utterances of their ancestors, and inherited awe, have rendered sacred. Here they celebrate the grim initiation of their barbarous rites with a human sacrifice for the good of the community.

This calls to mind particularly the Grauballe man who lay with his throat cut, the sign of a ceremony in which the sacrificial blood had to well out in a stream to the gods whom it was desired to honour. We do not know how the Grauballe man came to be chosen for sacrifice, or whether he was a servant in the holy places or an ordinary member of the community. His neat hands, however, unaccustomed to toil, suggest that he was not chosen from the body of the peasantry. He may have been picked by lot. Tacitus refers to this custom in a reference to prophesies and omens:

A branch cut from a fruit-bearing tree is divided up into small splinters. Each of these is marked with a distinctive sign, so that it can be distinguished from the others. They are then thrown blindfold and at random on to a white cloth.

This recalls the four inch long white slivers, completely stripped of bark, which lay under the woman found in Borre Fen. They could indicate a casting of lots which sealed her fate and brought her into the bog as a human sacrifice.

It has also been suggested that the sacrificial victims were people who had already been condemned to death in accordance with the law and after judgement, and that the death penalty in Germanic law was accordingly of religious origin, taking the form of a sacrifice. The offending person's crime had aroused the anger of the gods and this could only be appeased by the forfeiting of his life. Against this it has been argued that the anger of the gods was only aroused by offences against their own divinity, and to support this Adam of Bremen is cited. In his history of the Bishopric of Hamburg, written about A.D. 1070, he recounts how the English missionary, Walfred, broke the images of the god Thor in the temple at Uppsala and was promptly lynched and sunk in a hole in a marsh.

In a chapter dealing with old Germanic law Tacitus writes:

At the assembly it is also permissible to lay accusations and to bring capital charges. The nature of the death penalty differs according to the offence. Traitors and deserters are hung from trees; cowards, poor fighters and notorious evil-livers are plunged in the mud of marshes with a hurdle on their heads: the difference of punishment has regard to the principle that crime should be blazoned abroad by its retribution, but abomination hidden.

We do not know what happened to the traitors and deserters after they had been hanged, but their punishment must have taken place in the course of war-like activity, which might well have been an almost everyday state of affairs in the period with which we are dealing. When we read that some offenders were sunk in marshes or bogs and covered with hurdles, or interwoven branches, this recalls the man found in Borre Fen in 1948, who was covered and packed about with heather stems, and several other bog people who were found covered with branches.

Tacitus names a special punishment for adultery by women, but says nothing about male adultery. The adulterous woman had her hair cut off in the presence of her relatives and was then scourged out of the village. This calls to mind one of the bog people in particular, the young girl from Windeby, in Domland Fen. She lay naked in her grave in the peat, her hair shaved off, with nothing but a collar of ox-hide round her neck, and with bandaged eyes.

Tacitus' account makes it clear that the Germani recognized several different gods, both male and female, in the Early Iron Age. For this too we find support in the archaeological record. It may be therefore that the great variety of ways in which the dead were put into the bogs depends not only on

52 Bronze Age fertility-goddess. From the bog at Viksø

53 The Viksø goddess, with double neck-ring, seen from the back

differences in date but also upon which of the gods they were offered to.

So far as can be inferred from the archaeological finds of the Celtic Iron Age it was a goddess that was dominant in the northern circle of deities; and she already held this dominance in the last two phases of the Bronze Age. The sacrificial deposits of the bogs tell us that this goddess held sway at least two centuries before the Early Iron Age began. She is depicted in several small representations in bronze—a naked figure wearing only a pair of collars round her neck and rings in her ears, and with her hands held under her breasts—as the mother-goddess, the source of all—Mother Earth.

These figures obviously represent a fertility goddess, the goddess known to us in the ancient cultures of the Middle East as the old Asiatic goddess, Ishtar, or Astarte; and as the Greek goddess of love and fertility, Aphrodite; these being only two of a whole array of fertility goddesses.

She it is who plays the leading role in the great ritual drama, the purpose of which is to ensure the rhythm of the crops. The seed is buried, and sleeps in the earth the sleep of the dead; but in the spring it awakes and springs up to a new life and the promise of rich harvest.

She it is also who sees to the increase of cattle and the fruition of the creative act of love amongst men. In all the ancient agricultural civilizations, as here in the north, she is represented with her sex emphasized and her hands pressed against her life-giving breasts.

The drama acted out in the changing seasons of the year, death in the autumn, the winter's sleep and the spring re-awakening, was probably pictorially represented in the north as early as the Bronze Age. A comprehensive illustration of it, carved over 2,500 years ago, occurs on an ice-scoured rock at Tuvene in Bohuslän in Sweden. From right to left, we see a man wearing a horned helmet and carrying an axe—the killer. In the middle, under the representation of a ship or boat, the man lies asleep in the grip of winter. On the extreme left

54   The drama of the seasons, a rock-carving in Bohuslän, Sweden

the wakened man is shown in the act of love with the goddess of Spring.

The Danish Bronze Age is divided into six periods, and a study of the many hundreds of Bronze Age sacrificial deposits clearly shows the goddess gradually supplanting her male partner. In the first period masculine objects are supreme. In the second they represent only about 40 per cent of the material found, and in the fifth and sixth periods only 25 per cent and 10 per cent, whereas the percentage of feminine objects in these last two periods rises to 75 per cent and then 90 per cent. These statistics agree with the evidence of Bronze Age human representations. While male figures appear in the second period, female figures do not appear until the fourth. We should not place too much stress on the evidence of plastic representations of the human figure, since so few survive. We can none the less say that female subjects are far

55   The fertility goddess with neck-chain, carried in the form of
an amuletic ornament in the Stone Age

more numerous than male in the second half of the Bronze Age.

Yet this goddess was being worshipped as far back as the neolithic period, as we know from depictions of her on pottery vessels. She was carried in amulet form at the end of the Stone Age, although it is only the indicating of necklaces that tell us that she is concealed in the slender forms of these pendant ornaments carved from schist, a fine crystalline rock.

Torcs or necklets found in the bogs, often twisted like ropes, are evidence for the cult of this goddess, in the Bronze and Iron Ages alike. The torcs become so heavy in the Iron Age that they cannot all have been intended for human use. They were probably made specially as offerings for the goddess and deposited by women praying that they might have a child, or wanting to give thanks for a safe delivery.

Her symbol indicates how highly the goddess was esteemed in the Iron Age and how great the significance with which she was invested. It was worn as a brooch on the dress to ward off alien and hostile forces, just as the sign of the cross was worn in Christian times. Female amulets, which are known from both Jutland and the Danish islands, are highly stylized, but the sex is strongly emphasized in the breasts and belly, while the collars are merely indicated.

Tacitus in his *Germania* speaks of the goddess, who, he says, is worshipped by seven peoples, living between the rivers and the forests, who cannot be distinguished from one another in any way and who all worship Nerthus—Mother Earth—in common:

> In an island of the ocean is a holy grove, and in it a consecrated chariot, covered in robes. A single priest is permitted to touch it: he interprets the presence of the goddess in her shrine and follows with deep reverence as she rides away drawn by cows: then come days of rejoicing and all places keep holiday, as many as she thinks worthy to receive and entertain her. They make no war, take no arms; every weapon is put away: peace and quiet are then, and then

56　More than 300 bronze rings, deposited in Smederup bog
as an offering to the fertility goddess

57 Fertility goddesses in the form of amuletic ornaments
from the Iron Age

58 The sacred spring wedding, depicted in a rock carving in Bohuslän, Sweden

alone, known and loved, until the same priest returns the goddess to her temple, when she has had her fill of the society of mortals. After this the chariot and the robes, and, if you will believe it, the goddess herself, are washed in a sequestered lake: slaves are the ministrants and are straight-away swallowed by that same lake. Hence a mysterious terror and an ignorance full of piety as to what that may be which men only behold to die.*

The fertility rite which Tacitus describes is known to us from other areas of Indo-European civilization. It is the cycle of the sacred spring wedding, symbolizing the fruitful union of sky and earth, promoted by ritual celebration; the prelimi-naries are an awakening, journeyings through the country-side, days of peace and holiness while the journeys are in

* Loeb translation.

162

progress—then glad feasts of celebration, and, finally, human sacrifice. The worship of Nerthus did not only take place on the 'island of the ocean', which Tacitus writes about, but in sacred groves all over the country. This is made clear both by archaeological discoveries and by place-names. Tacitus' information was derived only from a single site.

Perhaps it is because of the dominating position of the goddess that Tacitus makes no mention of a male partner, essential in a ritual marriage. This role may have been performed by her priest, whose part in the ceremonies is so strongly emphasized by the Roman historian. The description of the drowning of the goddess's attendants in the lake on the completion of the rites recalls the sacrificed bog people. There is indeed much to suggest that the bog people were participants in ritual celebrations of this kind, which culminated in their death and deposition in the bogs.

Here one thinks of the special stamp of many of the bog people—delicate features and neat hands and feet, not worn by heavy work as those of soldiers and peasants must have been.

The dead man's last meal, taken perhaps half a day or a day before his sacrifice, also comes in for consideration here. It consisted of an abundance of just those grains and flower seeds which were to be made to germinate, grow and ripen by the goddess's journey through the spring landscape. In the three meals which it has so far been possible to analyse there has been not the slightest trace of summer or autumn fruits.

As noted in the chapter on the Grauballe man, there is thus reason to think that these Iron Age men met their deaths before spring began; and it is more plausible to suggest that they were given a special meal of the wild and cultivated plants of the district before being sacrificed to the spring goddess, than to suggest that they were vegetarians.

The rope nooses which several of the bog people carry round their necks, and which caused their deaths, are a further sign of sacrifice to the goddess, Nerthus. They are perhaps replicas of the twisted neck-rings which are the mark

59   The Borre Fen man, with his 'torc' or neck-ring

60 Two symbols of the same thing. The torc or neck-ring of the goddess,
and that of the Borre Fen man

of honour of the goddess, and a sign of consecration to her. The neck-ring is expressly the sign of the fertility goddess in this period. As we have seen, she is represented naked with a double twisted collar at the end of the Bronze Age. Dozens of pairs of bronze collars from this period have been found in the bogs, and the goddess with neck rings appears in several of the pictorial representations of the Celtic Iron Age. The rope noose round the dead bog man's neck should also be seen as a neck-ring and so as the pass which carries him over the threshold of death and delivers him into the possession of the goddess, consecrating him to her for all time. Thus we can speak of the skilfully plaited noose as the designating sign of the Tollund man, marking him out as consecrated to the goddess; likewise the curiously tied knot around the Borre man's neck, and the smooth hazel-withy round the neck of the man found at Windeby in the Domland fen. We know from western Nordic sources that hanging was used in this connection; it is recorded that one of the kings of the Yngling house in the Uppland province of Sweden, was hanged by his people as an offering to the corn goddess, to ensure a good harvest.

There exists a contemporary representation of the sacred ritual marriage which is the solemn climax of the goddess's spring journey. It was cut upon a flat stone some 2,500 years ago. We see a man and a woman, their sexual characteristics strongly emphasized, stretching out their arms to each other to clasp and unite. Behind the woman stands a tree, or perhaps an ear of corn, which marks her as the goddess of the burgeoning of spring. The whole scene is surrounded by the sacred sign of the goddess, the twisted collar, which here seems to have the look both of rope and of metal; but it may be intended for a wreath.

Many discoveries of carts or waggons, or of parts of them, support the evidence of the neck-rings and show that the peripatetic fertility goddess was worshipped in all parts of the country.

The discovery in the bog at Rappendam, in the north of

61   A spring wedding engraved on stone 2500 years ago

Zealand, is extremely illuminating; that from the bog of the
Manse at Dejbjerg in West Jutland the most splendid of such
finds.

At Rappendam—an elongated fen, once a lake, between
high banks—parts of no fewer than twenty-eight wheel
circles, four of which were complete, and along with them
thirteen hubs, were found during peat-cutting in 1941 and
1942. Some other parts of waggons were also recovered, and
the share of a plough, which was the agricultural tool of the

Early Iron Age. These objects lay in groups, indicating that they were deposited on a number of different occasions. Near one group was the skeleton of a man lying on his back with knees bent. The left arm was down by his side, the right lying obliquely across the chest, a posture known in many other bog people. Parts of the skeletons of at least five sheep and bones of cow, horse and wild pig were also found.

We can see at once that this is a sacrificial deposit which matches Tacitus' description. We have the carts, the draught animals and the human sacrifice—all three. It is the carts which give the sacrificial deposit its distinctive stamp. Not only are they not intact but broken into pieces, though in several instances they represent parts of waggons which had never been used and could not have been. We seem to be in the presence of a series of sacrificial deposits over many years, and that they were made specifically to the goddess Nerthus is perhaps also indicated by the parish name, Jørlinde, which is thought to contain the name of the fertility god, Njord, the male deity who took over the role of Nerthus in later antiquity.

This sacrificial site at Rappendam was probably the shrine of the peasantry. The one now to be described may have been that of the highest circles in the land.

The two waggons found in the bog belonging to the Manse of Dejbjerg, which were discovered in the 1880s, are perhaps the actual ones used to transport the goddess herself. The fine craftsmanship and the opulent decoration with bronze mountings and human masks show at any rate that these were not workaday carts like those from Rappendam, or even carts used by the Jutland peasants on more festive occasions. Several pottery vessels found with them show that they were deposited in the bog in Tacitus' time. A part from a loom found in one of the pots gives a feminine slant to this find. Not all the portions of the two sacrificed carts were preserved, but a ceremonial seat or seat of honour, for one person, belong to them, and it is so finely appointed that one can legitimately visualize the goddess sitting in it during her spring journeys through the villages of the district. The burnt Iron Age village of Fjande,

62 Cart sacrificed in Rappendam Fen

63 *and* 64 The Dejbjerg waggon and a 2500-years-old representation of the waggon of the goddess, drawn by oxen. (Rock-carving from Bohuslän.)

already referred to (p. 124), perhaps lay at the outer limit of the area covered by this waggon on its ritual spring journey.

It has been debated whether Nerthus was of Celtic or of Oriental origin. It does not matter for our purposes, for the northern and the Celtic fertility goddesses both have oriental prototypes. The goddess is to be seen in all her majesty, splendidly fashioned, on Celtic bronze and silver vessels offered sacrificially in Danish bogs. Although these vessels were not manufactured in Denmark, and show us the Celtic peoples' concept of their gods and goddesses, the rich world of pictorial imagery represented by the cauldrons cannot have failed to impress itself on the northern, Germanic, people also. They probably used these vessels for many years at their sacrificial celebrations and annual sacred rituals. Such sacred cauldrons must have constituted a significant part of the national wealth of the different tribal regions. They must have left a deep impression on the visual imaginations of their northern owners before they were themselves sacrificed in bogs in the wake of epoch-making-events, events perhaps even important in world history.

On the great bronze cauldron discovered in Rynkeby Fen, in the north of Fyn, in 1845, the goddess can be seen driving out with her team of oxen. The Rynkeby cauldron was presented to the Museum of Northern Antiquities by the Crown Prince, who later became so well-known as the archaeologist-king, Frederick VII.

The great silver cauldron from Gundestrup shows us gods and goddesses, cult processions, sacrificial scenes, animal combats, and indeed gives us a complete picture of a Celtic people's world of deities and of the rituals associated with their worship. It is a picture-world which even at the time when the cauldron was in use only the initiated priesthood could interpret, and at the meaning of which we now can only guess. The cauldron was found in the little pot-shaped bog of Raeve—not at its centre, but in front of the eminence which dominates the surrounding area, and from which one can see to the south over the expanse of Borre Fen to the spot where

65 Raeve Fen. The Gundestrup cauldron was found at the spot marked by the big stone

the two Iron Age women and the Iron Age man were found, and, at the southern extremity of the fen, to the fortified island and its village.

A large glacial boulder now marks the spot where the marvellous silver cauldron was found. Peat is no longer cut there. Gradually the banks have become overgrown with thickets of alder, willow, aspen and birch. In spring the great bank to the north, covered with broom in flower, is like a flaming pyre. On the flat surface of the bog an aromatic fragrance spreads from the low vegetation of bog myrtle, the pointed earth-green leaves of which served to satisfy the taste for beer in the bog people's day and are considered by modern connoisseurs to be one of the finest aromatic ingredients in good Danish brandy.

We cannot undertake here a full account of all the pictorial scenes on the cauldron, but will only mention some few details which throw light on the bog people. On one of the plates which decorated the interior of the cauldron we probably have a representation of the peripatetic goddess wearing her neck-ring. She is surrounded by fabulous animals, which tell us that the cauldron was made in the East Celtic area.

A goddess of love is represented on one of the outside plates. Her role is symbolized by the bird she holds in her hand, and around her are two birds and other figures. A female attendant is plaiting her hair and a second woman by her right elbow is wearing the same sort of dress that was worn by the woman from Huldre Fen. Above her there appears a dog, perhaps a sign that she is also the goddess of death, and bears both the colours of red and black.

This view is supported by the other figures on this plate, for below her breasts lie a dead man and a dead dog. Sacrifice of dogs is not unknown in the Early Iron Age, and a significant quantity of dog-bones, mostly jaw-bones, occur in a big find of sacrificed pots of this period in Vendsyssel.

All the goddesses on the Gundestrup cauldron wear torcs, as do some of the gods as well; but they also wear on their foreheads a woven band or one twisted like the neck-rings found

66 (*opposite*) The Gundestrup cauldron, with representations of gods and goddesses

67 The 'travelling' goddess on the Gundestrup cauldron, surrounded by fabulous animals

in the sacred groves, or the ropes round the necks of sacrificed bog men. The band on the forehead we recognize from the young woman of Domland Fen in Schleswig and from the chopped-off woman's head in Stidsholt Fen in Vendsyssel.

On one of its inner plates the Gundestrup cauldron probably depicts a man being sacrificed over a cauldron. Warriors pass in procession on either side of the tree of life which springs from the cauldron in which the sacrificial blood is collected. The lower row of warriors are on foot, perhaps prisoners of war about to be sacrificed, but the men of the upper row are on horseback, and they have been thought to represent the sacrificed men translated into new glory. That is why a dog, as the herald of death, meets the procession of the condemned, while a snake leads the riders forth. The vessel represented could also be regarded as a rejuvenation bath, rather than a cauldron for sacrifices, but this would not conflict with the general interpretation we have just suggested.

In his *Geography*, the Greek author Strabo describes the sacrifice of prisoners of war amongst the Cimbri. Strabo's *Geography* is a work of the time of Christ and contains information about the Germani:

> Among the women who accompanied their war-like expeditions were prophetesses who were also priestesses. They were grey with age, and wore white clothes and, over these, cloaks of the finest linen, and metal belts. They were barefoot. These women would enter the camp, sword in hand, and go up to prisoners, crown them, and lead them up to a bronze vessel which might hold some twenty measures. One of them would mount a step, and, leaning over the cauldron, cut the throat of a prisoner, who was held up over the vessel's rim. Others cut open the body and, after inspecting the entrails, would foretell victory for their countrymen.

The condition of the Gundestrup cauldron in the bog shows that it was a sacrificial offering and not buried as treasure, for it was in pieces and apparently deposited, like so many other offerings of the period, in an ancient peat-working. It lay a

68   A goddess, with symbols and woman attendants.
     From the Gundestrup cauldron

good twenty inches deep and without any protection. The
plates from the broken upper part of the cauldron were
placed in piles of five—one round bottom plate on top of four
of the others—in the great raised bowl which formed the
bottom part of the cauldron.

How did this magnificent silver cauldron come to the far
off land of the north Germanic peoples?

Why was it later deposited in the little sacrificial bog in the
heart of Himmerland?

We can of course only guess. When we consider the enor-
mous value that this vessel, unique in the world, must have
had two thousand years ago, it is possible that some event

69　Goddess with manly attributes on the Gundestrup cauldron

which left its mark on the history of the world lay behind it. The cauldron must have represented a considerable part of the wealth in silver of the entire population of Himmerland. As a sacred vessel it surpasses all others. I have myself related it to the wide-ranging migrations of the Cimbri through Europe, and explained it as booty sent home to the principal shrine in the heart of Himmerland, a shining trophy of the victories of kinsmen in foreign lands. But these victories gradually came to an end. Whole divisions of their army were cut down. When report of this reached the people at home they sought to change the fortunes of war, broke up the sacred vessel and gave it back to the gods in the condition that they required, if they were once more to lend their help towards victory.

70 Details from a sacrificial scene on the Gundestrup cauldron

The Iron Age peoples may have recognized traits of their native gods in these Celtic pictures on the great sacrificial cauldron, and perhaps even appropriated some of these deities wholly. But they themselves also made images of the gods, not in rare metals with a distinctive art-style, but in a material ready to hand—in wood.

In the summer of 1961 Harald Andersen uncovered at Foerlev Nymølle three sacrificial sites in the bog below the northern slope of the hill. They were close together and in each the finds were stones, potsherds, and worked wood. The three sites however had not been in use simultaneously, but probably, in the centuries B.C., at times separated by long intervals. In one of these sites the stones were gathered up in a heap, and under this heap of stones lay a cloven oak-branch nine feet in length—the goddess herself. The branch in itself possessed natural 'femine' form—suggesting a slender body, rounded hips and long legs and only the most distinctive features had been added by working or carving it. The sex was shown by a strong incision where the fork began. The roundness of the hips was emphasized by cutting back the upper part of the legs at both sides. Head, arms and feet were all lacking, and it is perhaps just because of this that the female character of the figure is so apparent.

This bog also produced a wooden club, several long ski-like planks of uncertain use and significance, and also a number of the pots that are so characteristic of Iron Age sacrificial sites in the bogs. In addition there were bones of animals—domestic ox, goat, sheep, dog, horse and hare. A badly disintegrated shoulder-blade showed that humans, too, gave their lives in the sacrificial celebrations dedicated to the goddess. Her significance as goddess of fertility is underlined by the presence of a bunch of flax placed upon the heap of stones under which she was preserved in the bog water when not needed for feast days. We can imagine her on these feast days, standing on her long legs, turned frontally to the worshipping Iron Age populace. The flax may indicate that people brought to this spot thank-offerings for a good harvest,

71 The Goddess Nerthus at Foerlev Nymølle

the outcome of the goddess's journeyings in the early spring.

Another goddess-figure was uncovered in 1946 in peat-cutting in a little bog near Rebild Skovhuse, in East Himmerland. It was saved for posterity by a museum official, Peter Riismøller. Here too the shape of the goddess was inherent in the grown wood, but the birch-branch with its swaying feminine curves, which provided the raw material, had also had its sex emphasized by an incision in the lap, four strongly-marked folds in the stomach, and a little cutting away to suggest the form of the head.

A large piece of woven cloth belonged to the goddess. She probably lay wrapped up in it in the sacred grove in the bog when she was not being carried around the Iron Age fields in the neighbourhood of Rebild Skovhuse in the role of the spring goddess, Nerthus.

The sex of this goddess-figure is perhaps not exclusively feminine but rather hermaphrodite; for we encounter the same deity a thousand years later in male form under the name of Njord, the fertility god of the Vikings. The farmer's wife who produced it to the Museum official evidently took it for a male figure, saying to Mr Riismøller: 'Here he is'.

It is clear that the goddess had a male partner, even though he is not mentioned by Tacitus. It may be that the robust image of a fertility god which came to light in 1880 in Broddenbjerg Fen, near Viborg, represents such a partner. Again the figure takes its form from the natural growth of the wood, but this form is distinctly male. The oak-fork from which it is fashioned has a side-branch jutting out at the point of bifurcation, and cut and worked so as to take on the characteristic features of a phallus. As in the case of the goddess-images, hands and feet are lacking; but a face, masculine in cast and full of character, was produced by very simple cuts.

The Broddenbjerg god was found in circumstances exactly similar to those in which the Nerthus figure at Foerlev Nymølle was found—amongst a heap of stones in a bog, along with deposited pottery vessels which confirm the date as Early Iron Age.

72   The goddess Freya at Rebild Skovmose

73 Representation of a god, with offerings of pottery vessels from Spangeholm

The discovery of a torc and armlets of Bronze Age date show that a female deity was also worshipped at the same bog—a circumstance paralleled in the extreme south of the Jutland peninsula, at Braak in Holstein. Here both a god and a goddess were found, executed in the same rudimentary wood-carving technique, in which the main forms were those of the natural growth of the wood.

The simplest of all the representations of male deities is the figure discovered in Spangeholm Fen, in Vendsyssel, standing in the midst of a sea of Iron Age pottery vessels. It is a powerful male organ, the most potent symbol of the fertility-god. It consists of a branch of oak twenty-six inches long with a knot at one end, the other having been sharpened so that it could be driven down into the bottom of the bog. There in the bog it stood to receive its share of the year's harvest, deposited in pottery vessels in a ring around the male deity erect in all his splendour. Year by year the number of vessels increased to twenty, thirty, forty and even more. This remarkable discovery can be seen in the Museum at Vendsyssel, whose curator, Holger Friis, carried out the investigation at the site.

The sacrificial sites at Foerlev Nymølle, Broddenbjerg and Spangeholm illustrate for us the simple shrines of the Jutland peasants of the Iron Age, where their offerings were made, and where a female and a male deity were worshipped, in the hope of promoting the prosperity and fertility of the peasant community. And so it was throughout the land in all peasant communities small and great; for what could be more important than fertility in field and stall?

Archaeological discoveries show that other gods besides those of fertility were worshipped in the Early Iron Age—for example, the god of war. In a small cauldron-bog lying between hills near Hjortspring Kobbel, on the island of Als, a remarkable Early Iron Age boat was excavated—a war-canoe some sixty-five feet long, with a steering oar, and filled with war-gear, such as iron swords, spearheads and shields; also with more everyday equipment, such as bowls, boxes and smiths' tools. The find was clearly sacrificial in character, as

74 *and* 75   The Broddenbjerg god

the discovery of a dismembered horse beneath the boat confirmed. Other places in the bog yielded the bones of a large dog, a puppy and a lamb. A find of weapons from Krogsbølle Fen, on the island of Fyn, belonging to this period, consists of iron swords and spearheads, which were dug up near a paved way. This find probably testifies to a battle on a causeway and the subsequent offering of the weapons of the vanquished.

Offerings to the god of war increase towards the end of the Roman Iron Age. A score of such finds of this period are known, from all parts of the country. Many of them are of great size, containing hundreds of weapons and other war-booty. One of the finds contained in addition three boats. These great sacrificial deposits of war-gear are evidence of troubled times and battles between great tribal areas, and also of the command of the war-god over men's minds. The finds show that he desired not only the weapons of the vanquished, but also richer spoils in the shape of silver helmets, coats of mail, Roman coins and fine raiment. Caesar writes of similar offerings amongst the Gauls:

> When they join battle they generally promise the spoils of war to the War God. After the victory captured animals are sacrificed to him and the rest of the booty is gathered up in one place. In many towns heaps of such things are to be seen piled up in sacred places. It is very rarely that anyone has so little respect for religion as to risk either the concealment of booty at home, or the removal of anything that has once been deposited as an offering. For this offence a terrible death is decreed.

As the great deposits of weapons represent sacrificial ceremonies for entire tribal areas, so the sacrifice of human beings, and the depositing of their bodies in sacred bogs, must also be the act of a large congregation. Feast days accompanied by human sacrifice attracted participants from all over the district, and special persons were selected as the sacrificial victims.

A story which reflects to some extent the fate of the Tollund man and other bog people is told in the Icelandic literary source, the Flatø book. It occurs in the saga of Olaf Tryg-vasson. The episode took place at the time when King Olaf held in court at Trondheim and charged the Viking chieftain Leif Eriksson with the task of proclaiming the Christian faith in Greenland. In the journey to Greenland, Leif drifted so far on the sea that he discovered a hitherto unknown land where there were fields of wild corn and where vines grew. This was America, which the northmen called 'Vinland'. It was at this time that the chieftain Gunnar Helming was suspected at Trondheim of a murder which someone else had, in fact, committed. Warned by his brother Sigurd, who was at Olaf's court, he succeeded in escaping eastwards, through forests and mountains, to Sweden. There the people were much given to great sacrificial celebrations, and the special object of their worship was the god Frey, who had as his attendant a pretty young woman. The peasants believed that Frey was a living person and that he needed a wife to sleep with. It was the duty of Frey's wife, in consultation with the god, to arrange everything to do with the sacrificial cele-brations.

Gunnar Helming finally approached Frey's wife, making out that he was a poor foreign traveller, and asked her for shelter. She told him that he was indeed an unlucky man, since the god Frey did not look on him with favour. Gunnar replied that he would rather have her help and favour than Frey's. As he was gay and lively, he managed to have his stay prolonged, until in the end Frey's wife said to him: 'The people like you, so I think it will be best if you stay the winter and take part with Frey and me in the festival when Frey ensures for the countryfolk a fruitful year. But Frey does not like you at all.'

When the time came for them to leave home, Frey and his wife took their places in a waggon, while their servants went in front. On the long journey through the mountains they were assailed by a storm, and Gunnar had to lead the horses. Finally all the servants fled. Gunnar was left alone with the

god and his wife, and when he became tired he got up into
the driving seat, but Frey's anger drove him out again. Finally
he started a fight with Frey, who had the upper hand until
Gunnar called for Christ's help; at this, the devil who inhabited the image of the god left it, and Gunnar was able to
break it in pieces.

Gunnar then told Frey's wife that he would abandon her if
she did not say, when they came to the villages, that he was
the god, and he put on Frey's clothing. When they arrived at
the first of the banquets, where a great crowd had gathered,
he won everyone's favour, because he had forced a passage
through the long mountain passes alone with his wife in such
weather; and, what was more, could eat and drink like other
men. They then moved from feast to feast, but Frey did not
speak much with anyone but his wife. Gradually, as time
passed, people began to notice that Frey's wife was with child,
and they thought this was splendid, all the more so because
the weather was so fair and everything seemed so full of
promise, as never before in living memory. The power of the
Swedish god of fertility was widely spread abroad and came to
the ears of King Olaf Trygvasson, who guessed the connection
and sent Sigurd to Sweden to help his brother escape—which
he did. The Swedes had also become suspicious; but they
lost their way in pursuing the fugitive, who had taken his
wife with him. We cannot doubt that this story of the fertility
god, coming down to us from Christian times, a thousand
years after the time of the bog people, was founded on fact.

At the beginning of the era of the bog people it was not a
male but a female god that was dominant; and her servant,
who fulfilled the role of the male deity, had to be sacrificed
at the completion of the journeyings so that the cycle of
nature might be supported and helped forward.

The Tollund man and many of the other bog men, after
their brief time as god and husband of the goddess—the time
of the spring feasts and the wanderings through the villages—
fulfilled the final demand of religion. They were sacrificed and
placed in the sacred bogs; and consummated by their death

76 The Tollund man sacrificed to the fertility goddess, Mother Earth, who has preserved him to our own day

the rites which ensured for the peasant community luck and fertility in the coming year. At the same time, through their sacrificial deaths, they were themselves consecrated for all time to Nerthus, goddess of fertility—to Mother Earth, who in return so often gave their faces her blessing and preserved them through the millennia.

Bibliography

(by chapters)

I The Tollund Man

1. Hans Helbaek, 'Tollundmandens sidste måltid' (The Tollund man's last meal), *Årbøger for Nordisk Oldkyndighed og Historie*, 1950
2. Knud Thorvildsen, 'Moseliget fra Tollund' (The Tollund bog man), *Årbøger for Nordisk Oldkyndighed og Historie*, 1950

II The Grauballe Man

3. P. V. Glob, 'Jernaldermanden fra Grauballe' (The Iron Age man from Grauballe), *KUML*,* 1956
4. Hans Helbaek, 'Grauballemandens sidste måltid' (The Grauballe man's last meal), *KUML*, 1958
5. Svend Jørgensen, 'Grauballemandens fundsted' (The site where Grauballe man was found), *KUML*, 1956
6. Carl Krebs and Erling Ratjen, 'Det radiologiske fund hos moseliget fra Grauballe' (The results of radiography of the body of the Grauballe man), *KUML*, 1956
7. G. Lange-Kornbak, 'Konservering af en oldtidsmand' (The conservation of a human body from antiquity), *KUML*, 1956
8. Willy Munck, 'Patologisk-anatomisk og retsmedicinsk undersøgelse af moseliget fra Grauballe' (The results of pathological and forensic tests on the body of the Grauballe man), *KUML*, 1956

* KUML is the annual publication of the Jysk Arkeologisk Selskab (Archaeological Society of Jutland) at Aarhus (Århus).

9. Henrik Tauber, 'Tidsfaestelse af Grauballemanden ved kulstof-14 måling' (The carbon-14 v.e. dating of the Grauballe man), *KUML*, 1956
10. C. H. Vogelius Andersen, 'Forhistoriske Fingeraftryk' (Prehistoric fingerprints), *KUML*, 1956

III Bog People in Denmark

11. J. Brandt, 'Planterester fra et moselig fra aeldre Jernalder (Borremose)' (Plant remains in the body of an Early Iron Age man from Borre Fen), *Årbøger for Nordisk Oldkyndighed og Historie*, 1951
12. Oldsag-Committeen, 'Bemaerknignger om et Fund af et mumieagtigt Kvinde-Lig i en Mose ved Haraldskjaer i Jyllan' (Notes on a mummified female body found in a peat-bog at Haraldskjaer, Jutland), *Annaler for Nordisk Oldkyndighed*, 1836–7
13. N. M. Petersen, 'Yderligere Bemaerkninger om Dronning Gunhilde' (Further observations on Queen Gunhild), *Annaler for Nordisk Oldkyndighed 1842–3*, Copenhagen, 1842
14. H. K. Rask, 'Det opgravne Lig' (The body exhumed at Haraldskjaer), *Morskabslaesning for Den Danske Almue*, No. 2, 1839 (Haraldskjaer)
15. Stuhr, 'Over det i Undeleff Mose fundne uforraadnede Menneskelegeme' (On the well-preserved body found in Undeleff Fen), *Antiqvariske Annaler*, Copenhagen, 1815
16. Elise Thorvildsen, 'Menneskeofringer i Oldtiden. Jernalderligene fra Borrmose i Himmerland' (Human sacrifice in Antiquity. The Iron Age bodies found in Borre Fen in Himmerland), *KUML*, 1952
17. Knud Thorvildsen, 'Moseliget fra Borremose i Himmerland' (The bog-people from Borre Fen in Himmerland), *Nationalmuseets Arbejdsmark 1947*, Copenhagen 1947

IV Bog People in Other Countries

18. Alfred Dieck, 'Die noch nicht geborgene Moorleiche von Bonsdorf, Kreis Celle, aus dem Jahre 1450 und die Moorleiche von Rieper Moor, Kreis Rotenburg (Hannover), gefunden im Jahre 1751 (The bodies found preserved in a peat-bog at Bonsdorf (Celle district) in 1450 and at Rieper (Rotenburg district, Hanover, in 1751), *Die Kunde*, 1947

19. Alfred Dieck, 'Zur Geschichte der Moorleichenforschung und Moorleichendeutung' (On the history of the study and interpretation of the bog people), *Jahresschrift für Mitteldeutsche Vorgeschichte*, vol. XLI–XLII, 1958

20. Alfred Dieck, 'Zum Hominidenmoorfunde' (The problem of the bog people), *Neue Ausgrabungen und Forschungen in Niedersachsen*, 1963

21. H. Handelmann and Ad. Pansch, 'Moorleichenfunde in Schleswig-Holstein' (Bog-bodies found in Schleswig-Holstein), Kiel, 1873

22. H. Hayen, 'Vom "Roten Franz" und anderen Moorleichen des Emslandes' (On 'Red Franz' and other bog people from the Ems region), *Jahrbuch des Emsländischen Heimztvereins*, vol. VI

23. Herbert Jankuhn, 'Ein Moorleichenfund aus dem Ruchmoor' (A body found in Ruchmoor), *Offa*, vol. III, 1938

24. Karl Kersten, 'Ein Moorleichenfund von Osterby bei Eckernförde (A bog body from Osterby near Eckernförde), *Offa*, vol. VIII, 1949

25. 'Lady Moira's Account of a Skeleton found in Drumkeragh in County Down', *Archaeologia*, vol. VII, pp. 90–110, London, 1785

26. Mestorf, 'Moorleichen' (Bog bodies), *Bericht des Schleswig-Holsteinischen Museums vaterländischer Altertümer*, Kiel, 1907

27. Karl Schlabow, 'Haartracht und Pelzschulterkragen der Moorleiche von Osterby' (The hair style and fur collar of the Osterby bog man), *Offa*, vol. VIII, 1949

28. Karl Schlabow, W. Hage and H. Jankuhn, 'Zwei Moorleichenfunde aus dem Domlandsmoor' (Two bodies from Domland Fen), *Praehistorische Zeitschrift*, vol. XXXVI, 1958

V How They Lived

29. H. C. Broholm, *Kulturforbindelser mellum Danmark og Syden i aeldre Jernalder* (Cultural contacts between Denmark and the Mediterranean in the Iron Age), Copenhagen, 1960

30. Johannes Brønsted, *Danmarks Oldtid. III Jernalderen* (Early Denmark. III. The Iron Age), Copenhagen, 1960

31. Margrethe Hald, 'Oldanske Tekstiler' (The textiles of ancient Denmark), *Nordiske Fortidsminder*, vol. V, Copenhagen, 1950

32. Margrethe Hald, *Jernalderens Dragt* (Iron Age costume), Copenhagen, 1962
   Gudmund Hatt, *Landbrug i Danmarks Oldtid* (Agriculture in ancient Denmark), Copenhagen, 1937

33. Hans Helbaek, 'Ukrudstfrø som Naeringsmiddel i førromersk Jernalder' ('The seed of weeds as food in the pre-Roman Iron Age'), *KUML*, 1951

34. Karl Schumacher, *Germanendarstellungen* (Pictorial representations of the *Germani*), Mainz, 1935

VI When Death Came

35. Harald Andersen, 'Hun er Moder Jord' ('She is the Earth Mother'), *Skalk*, No. 4, 1961

36. Anders Backsted, *Guder og helte i Norden* (Gods and heroes of Northern Europe), Copenhagen, 1963

37. Arthur Feddersen, 'To Mosefund' (Two bog finds), *Årboger for Nordisk Oldkyndighed og Historie*, 1881

38. P. V. Glob, 'Neues aus Vendsyssels älterer Eisenzeit (Spangeholm)' (New Iron Age finds from Vendsyssel (Spangeholm)), *Acta Archaeologica*, vol. VIII, p. 190

39. Ole Klindt-Jensen, *Gundestrupkedelen* (The Gundestrup cauldron), Copenhagen, 1961

40. Georg Kunwald, 'Nogle Offerfund fra Nordsjaellandske Moser (Rappendam), (Some offerings found in the peat-bogs of North Zealand), *Frederiksborg Amt. Årbog* 1940, Hillerød, 1950

41. Henry Petersen, *Vognfundene i Dejbjerg Praestegaardsmose* (Waggons found in the Praestegaard bog at Dejbjerg), 1888

42. Peter Riismøller, 'Froya fra Rebild' (The goddess Freya from Rebild), *KUML*, 1952

43. G. Rosenberg, 'Hjortspringfundet' (The Hjortspring find), *Nordiske Fortidsminder*, vol. III, Copenhagen, 1937

44. Albert Sandklef, *Bockstensmannen och hans olycksbröder* (The Bocksten man and his brothers in misfortune), Stockholm, 1943

45. Foke Ström, *Nordisk hedendom. Tro och sed i förkristen tid* (Nordic paganism. Pre-Christian beliefs and customs), Göteborg, 1961

46. Jan de Vries, *Altgermanische Religionsgeschichte*, I–II (History of primitive Germanic religions), 1956–7

47. Jan de Vries, *Keltische Religion* (Celtic religion), Stuttgart, 1961

BIBLIOGRAPHY

LIST OF AUTHOR'S WORKS ON RELATED SUBJECTS*

1. *Eskimo Settlements in Kempe Fjord and King Oscar's Fjord*, 1935
2. *Danske Oldtidsminder*, 1942
3. *Etudes sur la Civilisation des Sépultures individuelles du Jutland*, thesis, 1944
4. *Eskimo Settlements in North-East Greenland*, 1946
5. *Ard and Plough in Prehistoric Scandinavia*, 1951
6. *Danish Antiquities, Late Stone Age*, 1952
7. *Danske Oldtidsminder*, 1967
8. *Al-Bahrain: De Danske Ekspeditioner til Oldtidens Dilmun*, 1968

* See also pp. 193, 196.

Index

Plate references are in italic type

INDEX

fishing, 124, 125
Fjande, Nissum fjord, 124, 168
flax, 133, 180
Foerlev Nymølle, 180; *71*
food (and drink), 32, 33, 35, 56, 57, 91,
    113, 122, 163, 173; funerary, 138, 146;
    sacrificial, 146
fortification, 125; *42; see* Borre Fen
Fraeer Fen, 80
Frey, 189 *et seq.*
Freya, 182
Friis, Holger, 185
funeral mounds, *see* buria
Funder Kirkaby, 28

Germani, *see* Caesar, Tacitus, Strabo
Germania, see Tacitus
Germany, 31, 101 *et seq.*, 147, 152, 153
Ginderup, Thy, 127 *et seq.*
glass beads, 25, 68, 69; vessels, 136, 138;
    49
gold, 25, 127, 136, 146; *44*
Grauballe, 37 *et seq.*, 141, 152, 163; *9–20*
grave goods, 134, 135 *et seq.*, 145 *et seq.; 48–
    50*
Greek contacts, 128, 131, 138, 147
Gundestrup, 119; cauldron, 44, 83, 86, 133,
    151, 171 *et seq.; 65–70*
Gundhild, Queen, 70 *et seq.; 22*
Gunnar Helming, 189 *et seq.*
Gunnelsmose, 70

Hald, Dr Margrethe, 129
Halland, Sweden, 148
hair, 20, 25, 31, 37, 48, 66, 68, 74, 77, 82,
    90, 91, 98, 100, 105, 110, 112, 117, 146,
    153; *26, 33, 34, 41*
halter, *see* noose
Hamburg, 101
hanging, 20, 25, 32, 90, 96, 105, 144, 151,
    153, 166; *see* noose
Hansen, H., 20, 22
Harald, King, 70, 72
Haraldskjaer, 70, 73, 77, 80, 105; *22*
Hatt, Prof. Gudmund, 124
head, 116; *see* decapitation; *41*
hearths, 122, 127, 128
Helbaeck, Dr Hans, 32
Hesselhus, 24
Hingst Fen, Kreepen, 105
Hjortspring Kobbel, Als, 185
Hoby, Lolland, 136; *48*
Holland, 101, 104, 110,
houses, 121 *et seq.*
Hørby Fen, Himmerland, 98
Huldre bog, Ramten, 79, 80, 129, 134,
    173; *24, 25*
human sacrifice, 20, 25, 32, 48, 57, 59, 144,
    147 *et seq.*, 151, 152, 162 *et seq.*, 176, 180
Hverrestrup, 119

Icelandic sagas, 189 *et seq.*
inhumation, 136, 144 *et seq.*
Ireland, 101, *see* Drumkeragh
Iron Age, *passim*

Jørgensen, Dr Svend, 42
Jørlinde, 168
Juthe Fen, Jutland, 70

Karlbyneder in Dursland, 96
Kiel Museum, 107
Klosterlund, 24
Kohlmoor, Osterby, 116; *41*
Kongens Thisted, 119
Kragelund Fen, 25, 96
Krebs, Prof. Carl, 48
Krogsbølle Fen, Fyn, 188

Landegge, 104
Lange-Kornbak, G., 58
linen, 133
Lisbjerg cemetery, *50*
Little Binderup, 119
Lolland chieftain, 136; *48*
loom, 128, 168;—weights, 128
lot, choice of victims, 93, 152
lurs, 44
Lykkegård Fen, 96

magic, 124; *see* superstition
Masurian lakes, 101
Mesolithic period, 101
Mestorf, Johanna, 107
Moira, Lord and Lady, 103
money, 25, 127, 146; *44*
mosaic, 128
Mother Earth, *see* Earth Mother
Munck, Prof. Willy, 45
Museums, *see* Aalborg, Aarhus, Assen,
    Copenhagen, Kiel, Northern Antiquities,
    Schloss Gottorp, Silkeborg, Sønderborg
    Castle, Vendsyssel, West Himmerland
mutilation, 144

National Museum, *see* Copenhagen
Nebelgård Fen, 37, 42
Nederfrideriksmose, *21*
Neolithic, 159
Nerthus, *see* Earth Mother
Nielsen, Peter, 20
Nielsen, S. V., 86, 87, 93
Njord, 168, 182
noose, 20, 32, 90, 96, 163 *et seq.; 7, 29, 60;*
    see hanging
Northern Antiquities Museum, 171
Norway, 101

Odense, Church of St Knut, 83
Odin, 143
Olaf Trygvasson saga, 189 *et seq.*
ornaments, 25, 68, 69, 91, 104, 129, *et seq.*,
    134 *et seq.*, 145, 146, 159; *49, 55–7, 60*
Orosius, Paul 141
Osterby, 116, 117

peasants, 124, 127, 168; *50; see* social
    status
pinning-down body, 66, 74, 77, 80, 87, 91,
    104, 105, 112, *et seq.*, 149, 153; *23, 38*
plants, cultivated, 33, 35, 44, 56, 91, 122,

199